DOUBLE-O DINING

DOUBLE-O DINING

A JAMES BOND COOKBOOK

EDWARD BIDDULPH

BearManor Media
2022

Double-O Dining: A James Bond Cookbook

© 2022 *Edward Biddulph.*

All rights reserved.

Published in the United States of America by:

BearManor Media

4700 Millenia Blvd.
Suite 175 PMB 90497
Orlando, FL 32839

bearmanormedia.com

Printed in the United States.

Typesetting and layout by BearManor Media

Front cover: James Bond and Dominique Derval dining at the Café Martinique in Thunderball (1965). Artwork by Billy Robertson

ISBN—978-1-62933-929-0

Table of Contents

To

KIM BIDDULPH

Muse

Acknowledgements

I am hugely grateful to Ben Ohmart for his advice and the opportunity to publish my cookbook with Bear Manor Media, and to Stone Wallace for his deft editing. I would also like to thank Andrew Lycett for writing the foreword. Just as Ian Fleming had his heroes, I have mine, and Andrew is certainly in that category. His biography of Ian Fleming is a constant reference and has shaped my view of Ian Fleming's world like no other work about the author.

I would also like to thank the many readers of my previous book, *Licence to Cook*, and visitors to my website, *James Bond Food*, who have tried my recipes and provided feedback, and others who have given me information and encouragement over the years. It is impossible to name them all, but I would especially like to thank Paul Atkinson, Ajay Chowdhury, Tom Cull, Alice Dryden, David Leigh, David Lowbridge-Ellis, James Page, Jon Pettigrew, Matt Sherman, Graham Thomas, and Frieda Toth. Needless to say, any errors in the book are my responsibility alone.

I owe an enormous debt of gratitude to Clare McIntyre and Clare Abbott for the wonderful food photography. I am grateful, too, to my brother, Radley, who contributed the doughnut and plum pudding recipes and provided some very useful references. Finally, but by no means least, I would like to thank my wife Kim and daughter Katharine for their unwavering support, patience and willingness to eat just about anything I placed before them.

All recipes in this cookbook derive from recipes which first appeared in *Licence to Cook* (2010) or the website jamesbondfood.com, published between 2019 and November 2021.

Foreword

Ian Fleming stated clearly in his 1963 novel *On Her Majesty's Secret Service* that James Bond was no gourmet. However, 007 was certainly what we would today call a foodie. He loved his nosh; he was knowingly, almost smugly, informed about its provenance; and he always chose well from any menu put before him, much in the manner of Fleming himself.

Of course, Bond is more renowned for his drinking (that vodka martini "shaken not stirred"). But food has always featured strongly in his exploits, even if, as Edward Biddulph establishes in these pages, there's less of it in the films than in the books.

In print the secret agent's culinary preferences are often lovingly detailed. The process starts with breakfast, his favourite meal of the day, and in particular with scrambled eggs, the dish that he and his creator enjoyed above all others. Bond, or rather Fleming's Bond, has a bit of a fetish about eggs. If not scrambled, then fried will do, but preferably four of them because that, according to his creator, "has the sound of a real man's meal". In a pinch boiled can pass muster, but the single (007 is particular about that) egg should be dark-hued, from a Marans hen.

And, this being Fleming whose success was based appreciably on his ability to reflect the aspirations of a generation beginning to embrace the wider world after the deprivations of the war, Bond likes specific brands of produce, such as marmalade (Frank Cooper's Vintage Oxford) and coffee (preferably very strong—the Blue Mountain from Jamaica is mentioned—brought from de Bry in New Oxford Street and brewed in an American Chemex). He often rounds off his meal with fruit, the more exotic the better, such as papaya or pawpaw when in the Caribbean or the figs with yoghurt that Bond enjoys in Istanbul in *From Russia With Love*, and he is usually ready to try local specialities, including the salt fish and ackee which are ubiquitous and so delicious in Jamaica.

Edward Biddulph has seized on this material to tell an engaging piece of social and cultural history which passes under the cover of a traditional cookbook. Blessed with an encyclopaedic knowledge of James Bond's habits, whether in print or on the screen, he has combed the canon and noted anything non-liquid that passed Bond's lips. He has sourced these items, tested the dishes in his own kitchen, and served up each rich and tasty concoction, with generous sides of astuteness and wit.

Thus, when Biddulph refers to Peking Duck, a Bond favourite, he knows not only that Ian Fleming enthused about the dish when he ate it in Hong Kong, as part of a meal recorded in his book *Thrilling Cities* (1961), but also that Sean Connery reflects fondly upon it at the start of the film *You Only Live Twice* (1967).

But Biddulph's particular skill is to relate such information to what goes on in the kitchen, and in distinctly Bondian terms. So, since the skin of Peking Duck needs to be thoroughly dried, and brandy, vodka, or some other form of alcohol is often used as a desiccant, Biddulph suggests (and has clearly tried) using Bond's signature vodka martini in the formula laid out by Fleming in his 1954 novel *Live and Let Die*. When honey is required for the duck's basting sauce, Biddulph knows his canon well enough to suggest using Bond's favourite—heather honey, ideally from Norway.

Bond's travels allow Biddulph to call on a wide range of cuisines. Yet, however unusual certain items might once have been, they are now remarkably accessible and egalitarian. One only has to look at the 'triple a' vegetables—asparagus, artichoke and avocado—mentioned by Biddulph. These may have been prohibitively expensive and near unobtainable in 1952 (when Fleming wrote his first novel *Casino Royale* in Jamaica) but they are reasonably priced supermarket fare seventy years later.

Bond's gastronomic preferences would not feature in any modern book of cholesterol-free fare. They are often (but not always) heavy on butter and fat, with a marked and anachronistic taste for sauces. But they are excitingly cosmopolitan, showing evidence of Fleming's own journeying in foreign lands—particularly in France where he (like Bond) made a point a sampling the excellent menus in restaurants attached to railway stations. There is not much from Germany and Austria—surprisingly, as Fleming spent several formative years there. But this absence is compensated by input from other favoured Fleming destinations, notably the United States.

Biddulph takes obvious care in getting every detail right. He has spent a lot of time at his stove perfecting the dishes he writes about. He then fleshes them out with pieces of related information. I was struck by the way he checked Fleming's Jamaican references against recipes he himself found in local papers such as the *Daily Gleaner* and details of American dishes against contemporary menus found in archives located in the New York Public Library.

On a personal level I must add how happy I am to contribute an introduction to a cookbook which is rather different to what I usually write. But then even a basic knowledge of James Bond and Ian Fleming allows one to accumulate and sometimes show off unexpected expertise. I've lectured on automobiles. Next up perhaps a book on drink. And in the meantime, this culinary assortment is a true delight, to be savoured and tried out in your own kitchen.

Andrew Lycett, author of *Ian Fleming: The Man Behind James Bond* (1995, Turner Publishing, Inc., Atlanta)

1. How to Eat Like James Bond

"We all have our secrets," James Bond (Daniel Craig) tells Madeleine Swann (Léa Seydoux) in *No Time to Die* (2021), and this cookbook reveals a few of its own. The first secret has been hiding in plain sight since the first film, *Dr. No*, in 1962: food is as much a part of the film series as the vodka martinis, the globe-trotting locations, the gadgets, and fast cars. You don't believe me? Well, what does James Bond (Sean Connery) sing as Honey Ryder (Ursula Andress) emerges from the sea onto the beach in *Dr. No*? "Underneath the Mango Tree," which in its lyrics also lists banana, tangerine, sugar, ackee and cocoa beans.[1] In *From Russia with Love* (1963), James Bond (Sean Connery again) spies a wrong 'un when Grant (Rob-

A vodka martini. We all know what James Bond drinks, but what does he eat? Photo: Clare McIntyre

ert Shaw) orders red wine with fish. Food is essential to Blofeld's (Telly Savalas) diabolical scheme to spread a deadly virus and wage biological warfare in *On Her Majesty's Secret Service* (1969). In *Diamonds Are Forever* (1971), villain Mr. Wint (Bruce Glover) literally get his just desserts when James Bond (you guessed it: Sean Connery) thrusts an explosive *bombe surprise* between his legs and hoicks him over the side of the ocean liner. Villains throw oysters down their throats and wrestle with cooked lobsters. Then there's the fruit. Every film has a big bowl of fruit somewhere in the proceedings. Bananas, oranges, grapes, mangoes, pineapples; they're all there, typically in hotel rooms and restaurants.

What's more, we get a view of people's kitchens in the Bond films as often as we see inside public conveniences and bathrooms (which is quite a lot). In *Live and Let Die* (1973), we're privileged to have a peek inside James Bond's (Roger Moore) kitchen. What does the kitchen in that film tell us about the spy who lives there? The focus of the kitchen scene is, of course, the space-age coffee machine. Today, espresso machines can be found in almost every home, but in 1973, such machines were a rare luxury. That doesn't stop Bond from being rather sloppy with M's drink, mind; Bond hands M a cup with a pool of coffee in the saucer. On the side, next to some bottles of wine and Champagne, there's another gadget that, at the time, would have been state-of-the-art. I would love to say that it's a toasted sandwich maker, but it's more likely to be a waffle maker. Along the back wall we can see a fridge-freezer and what looks like jars of biscuits or sugar or something like that on top. Next to the fridge on the worktop is a collection of rather nice copper kitchen ware: a serving plate or tray, a food warmer, a coffee-pot, and that mainstay of 1970s' dinner parties, a fondue set. The copper theme continues opposite with the extractor fan (or range hood) above the hob and oven, and we can just about see a large copper saucepan. On the other side of the coffee machine, there is a small dining table set for two, complete with two sets of glasses and salt and pepper-pots. What appears to be missing is food, but it's not entirely absent. There is a pineapple and some bananas—a foreshadowing of Bond's Caribbean adventure, perhaps—next to the coffee machine and what looks like wooden boxes next to the copper ware that may contain eggs or vegetables, and presumably the fridge contains something of sustenance.

This is a spacious, shiny, underused kitchen that would be the pride of any kitchen showroom. It's a kitchen designed for intimate evenings with beautiful Italian agents and small, sophisticated gatherings where Bond can show off his latest gadgets. It's certainly not a place for serious, everyday cooking. Apart from waffles and fondue (hardly staple items), the best that Bond might be able to manage is scrambled eggs cooked in the copper pan, and I wouldn't be surprised if the fridge contained some cold cuts of meat or other items that wouldn't take much preparation. The kitchen is built for someone who doesn't spend a lot of time in it, but nevertheless desires the best equipment going. It is, in short, the perfect kitchen for spies like James Bond.

The paucity of food in James Bond's kitchen is something of an exception among the film series' kitchen scenes. In other kitchens, food is very much in evidence. Take the kitchen of the MI6 safe-house at Blayden in *The Living Daylights* (1987), the scene of a brutal fight between Necros (Andreas Wisniewski) and Blayden's butler (Bill Weston). While our eyes are firmly glued to the scrap itself, the attention to detail in the set design is such that we know what Blayden's residents are having for breakfast, what they're probably going to have for lunch, and what ingredients the kitchen staff have to hand. Apart from the fact that the milk has just been delivered, we know it's breakfast time because sausages and bacon are sizzling away on the grill. Eggs are also on the menu. A large egg-poacher sits on the hob, and if there are not boiled eggs in the saucepan of boiling water already, the eggs, which are on a counter near the other door, are about to go in. Cartons of orange juice can be found on a counter by the wall. Before he was interrupted by Necros, the chef (Michael Percival) began to carve a ham and had been rolling out some pastry. Ham pie for lunch? Cured sausages and fresh herbs hang beside the door frame, while boxes of fruit and vegetables sit on the floor in the corner. Next to the hob and grill are onions, green and red peppers, aubergines and cucumbers. The peppers and cucumbers may be going into a lunchtime salad, together with the lettuce by the sink that's waiting to be washed or has been washed and is draining. There are all sorts of store-cupboard basics around the kitchen, among them bottles of olive oil and vinegar of some description and, by the door the butler came through, what appears to be a comprehensive array of herbs and spices.

Then there's the kitchen of Margaret Thatcher (Janet Brown) at the end of *For Your Eyes Only* (1981). In what would have been quite a typical British kitchen, there is a toaster, scales, a rolling pin, a blender, storage jars of sugar and coffee and some pots and pans. We see, also on the worktop, a loaf of bread that's been sliced, a colander of the aforementioned sprouts, a dish of something reddish-brown (tomatoes or cocktail sausages?) and a bowl of eggs. The cupboard behind Mrs. Thatcher as she speaks on the phone contains boxes of cereal, as well as a range of larder items—flour, perhaps, and various tins and jars.

I could go on. The point is, there's plenty of food in the James Bond films; it's just that it's usually in the background and we don't see James Bond eat an awful lot of it. Ian Fleming's novels, however, are an entirely different matter. Food is mentioned in almost every chapter and it's usually Bond eating it, from breakfast—his favourite meal of the day—to dinner, for which Bond takes "a ridiculous pleasure."[2] The tone is set by the first novel, *Casino Royale* (1953), in which Bond's consumes, at the Hotel Splendide in the fictional French seaside resort of Royale-les-Eaux, a meal that commences with caviar, moves onto a very small beef tornedos with sauce Béarnaise, accompanied by a single artichoke heart, and ends improbably with half an avocado with French dressing.[3] The meal is very precisely described, and for Fleming's readers in 1950s' Britain, it must have been the last word in sophistication. This was, after all, a country where wartime rationing, with all its monotony and deprivations, was only just coming to an end and where avocados were almost unknown (and even when they were available, no one knew what to do with them[4]). Subsequent novels continued to whet readers' appetites with descriptions of sumptuous dishes eaten in glamorous locations. In the opening chapter of *Live and Let Die* (1954), James Bond, having arrived in New York, tucks into a meal of soft-shell crabs, hamburgers, french fries, broccoli, a mixed salad, and ice-cream with butterscotch sauce, and later, in Jamaica, breakfasts on a pawpaw, red banana, purple star-apples, tangerines, scrambled eggs and bacon.[5] In *Goldfinger* (1959), again in the opening pages of the book, Bond is sitting down in Miami to a dish of stone crabs dripping with melted butter.[6] Flick through the other books and it won't be long before you find meals of lobsters, Dover sole, lamb cutlets, beef steaks, and more caviar mouth-wateringly described. If Bond's exotic destinations turned Fleming's readers into armchair tourists, then descriptions of the food and wine gave them the language of the worldly gastronome. Ian Fleming stated that he wanted to stimulate his readers down to their taste buds,[7] and boy, did he succeed.

It is no secret that James Bond's diet is near-identical to that of his creator, whose socially and financially affluent lifestyle—with at least two months each year spent in Jamaica—gave him access to a range of food that, while normal to him, was far from the everyday experience of the book-buying public. Lunch for Ian Fleming at Scott's restaurant in London usually comprised grilled sole, which is also a favourite of Bond's while between missions in London.[8] A trip to Miami Beach in 1948 saw Fleming eat stone crabs, which Bond would eat 11 years later.[9] In Tokyo, both Fleming and Bond consume sukiyaki.[10] In Las Vegas, Fleming enjoyed charcoal-broiled steaks, just as Bond does subsequently during a mission to infiltrate a gang of diamond smugglers.[11] In New York Fleming and Bond go wild over the creamy oyster stew accompanied by a Miller's High Life beer and served at the Oyster Bar in Grand Central station.[12] In 1954, after travelling through Europe, Ian's wife Ann wrote how she and Ian had enjoyed "a high standard of cooking" and "a variety of menu."[13]

Oyster stew, crackers, and Miller High Life beer, consumed by both James Bond and Ian Fleming. Photo: Clare McIntyre

James Bond certainly enjoys good food and a varied menu in the books, but that's not to say that he dines only at the best restaurants, with food cooked by the top chefs. On occasion, Bond's food can be really quite normal and egalitarian, and that's the second secret highlighted in this cookbook. A loaf of bread and cured sausage bought from a local shop, various sandwiches, Welsh rarebit, fried eggs and ham, plain rice with flakes of fish, scrambled eggs: all basic, simple food that Bond consumes and enjoys during his adventures. Nor is Bond necessarily highly knowledgeable about food. With British, Jamaican, and French food, he's on safe ground. Give Bond a menu from a restaurant in London, Kingston or Paris, and he'll tell you exactly what he wants and how it wants it. From a gastronomic point of view, all three are his home turf. In the more unfamiliar surroundings of New York, Istanbul, and Tokyo, however, he allows his hosts—Felix Leiter, Darko Kerim Bey and Tiger Tanaka, respectively—to guide his food choices.[14] In fact, they choose for him. James Bond would never allow this in the films. Witness the dinner scene between Bond (Roger Moore) and Kristatos (Julian Glover) in *For Your Eyes Only* (1981), in which Bond rejects Kristatos's wine suggestion—a white wine from Kristatos's home region no less—in favour something less scented. Nevertheless, both the books and the films demonstrate an important principle of James Bond's food: Bond eats local and is open to new foods. No sticking (or rarely sticking) with the tried and tested for Bond; he, and by extension readers and viewers, experience regional ingredients and flavours.

This brings us to the third secret: the food of the James Bond books has never been so accessible and affordable as it is now. Just as the world has become smaller with cheap flights and 24-hour news reporting, so too have regional and national cuisines become part of our everyday dining. Restaurant chains offering all the foods of the world line the streets of city centres, and cavernous supermarkets, and even small, local convenience stores are well-stocked with foods—steak, asparagus, lobster and smoked salmon, among many other items—that appear in the Bond books. Indeed, James Bond's eating habits anticipated later gastronomic trends. Curry, spaghetti Bolognese, sushi, health foods, Continental-style breakfasts, exotic fruits, all consumed by Bond, are enormously popular today. For modern readers, Bond's diet might seem less sophisticated and luxurious, than commonplace and even quaint.

A word about the nutritional composition of James Bond food. A simple reading of the Bond books would suggest that Bond's diet isn't a well-balanced one. If we were to break his food items into component parts, we'd find that proteins (meat, fish, eggs and the like) form a very heavy part of his diet, with carbohydrates (potatoes, pasta, rice and so on), dairy, and fruit and vegetables accounting for relatively little. That might go some way to explaining Bond's slim build and body mass index of 22.69.[15] We needn't be too concerned, however, as descriptions of food in the novels may be deceptive. Mundane items such as vegetables, which accompany many meals as standard, may have escaped remark, the important point of note being the cut of meat or the piece of seafood. A steak that James Bond has in Las Vegas, for example, appears to have been ordered without vegetables, but Ian Fleming's account of his own visit to the city reveals that salads arrived with the steak as a matter of course.[16]

This cookbook reveals the final secret: how to cook the food of James Bond. In this volume, you'll find the answers to the enduring mysteries of the books and films. How do you cook brizzola? What is salade utopia? What's goes into quiche des cabinet? The answers to these questions and more, as well as inspiration for the recipes themselves, have come from various sources, not least the writings of Ian Fleming and others of his time and world, newspapers, and contemporaneous food descriptions. This reflects my own background. By profession I'm an archaeologist, not a chef, and in my job, I uncover evidence, sieve through it and piece it together to gain an understanding of the world in the past. Similarly, I have dug into the archives and other sources to gain an understanding of James Bond's world. This evidence has been carefully studied to create recipes that evoke a sense of period and give authenticity to the experience of eating like James Bond and, in some cases, the supporting cast—villains, friends and lovers.

One final note: since, when he is not alone, James Bond tends to dine with one other person (never, it seems, in a group), quantities specified in the recipes are usually for two people. These can of course be scaled up if the occasion demands. Almost all ingredients listed in the recipes are obtainable in the high-street supermarket. If items cannot be found there, specialist stores should fill the gaps, and if all else fails, there are suggestions for alternative ingredients. The cookbook is arranged by principal food category—meat and poultry, seafood, vegetables and so on—with recipes generally listed in alphabetical order by the terms by which they're described in the books or films. Dishes and ingredients can also be found using the index. Enjoy preparing the recipes. You now have a double-O number in dining, a licence to cook!

2. Egg and Cheese Dishes

Boiled Egg

Breakfast at home for James Bond includes a single boiled Marans egg in a blue eggcup with gold rim by Minton. Photo: Clare Abbott

James Bond may insist on three scrambled eggs, but boiled, he requires only one. An egg from a Marans hen, a particular favourite of his, may be difficult to find outside specialist-breed farm shops; it has a speckled or crazed appearance and has a dark brown, almost mahogany, colour. However, as Bond dislikes white eggs in general, any brown variety is suitable.[1]

Serves 1

1 egg

Place the egg in a small saucepan. Fill with enough water to cover the egg. Bring the water to the boil, setting the egg timer for 3 minutes and 20 seconds as the water's heating up. When the water begins to boil—for me, that's when large bubbles continuously form and break the surface of the water—start the timer. At the end of the cooking time, under a running cold water tap, carefully pour the water from the pan and at the same time cool the egg until you can pick the egg up by hand. Place the egg point-end down in the egg cup (blue with gold band and made by Minton, preferably).

Cheese Soufflé

Cheese soufflé, from the novel of *Goldfinger* (1959).
Photo: Clare McIntyre

The cheese soufflé that terminates James Bond's dinner with Goldfinger in the novel of *Goldfinger* (1959),[2] though somewhat unusual now, is a nod to the tradition, particularly in Britain, of serving savoury food at the end of the meal, which is claimed to cleanse the palette before drinking sweet or fortified wines. That would certainly explain the avocado with French dressing that ends James Bond's meals in *Casino Royale* (1953) and *Diamonds are Forever* (1956), and the marrow bone with which M finishes his meal at Blades in *Moonraker* (1955).[3]

In the film of *Octopussy* (1983), however, during dinner with Kamal Khan (Louis Jourdan) at his Monsoon Palace in India, the soufflé James Bond (Roger Moore) tucks into is where it more usually is these days: at the start of the meal.

Wherever they're placed, soufflés strike fear into the heart of many an inexperienced cook, but in reality they're very simple; the hard work is whisking the egg whites into stiff peaks.

Serves 2

½ oz./15 g. butter, plus a little more for greasing
½ oz./15 g. plain flour
⅜ cup/75 ml. milk
2 eggs
1 oz./25 g. Cheddar cheese, grated
Pinch of salt

Heat the oven to 400°F (200°C/180°C fan-assisted) and grease two ramekins with butter. Separate the eggs and beat the yolks.

Melt the butter in a saucepan and combine it with the flour to create a smooth paste. Pour in the milk and stir until the sauce thickens. Remove from the heat and leave to cool.

Whisk the egg whites until they're stiff. Stir the egg yolks, cheese and salt into the sauce, then gently fold in whites. Pour the mixture into the ramekins and place in the oven for 25 minutes.

Remove the soufflés from the oven and serve immediately.

Eggnog

At Christmas time, my thoughts naturally turn to the story of a remarkable man who redeemed a troubled soul, conquered evil, and saved the world. I refer, of course, to James Bond (George Lazenby) and his Yuletide adventure in the Swiss Alps. When we approach Christmas, what better way to get into the spirit of the season than to watch *On Her Majesty's Secret Service* (1969).

As for that perfect Christmas accompaniment, the answer is in the film. "Eggnog on Christmas Eve. Just like home," says the English girl (Joanna Lumley) as the Angels of Death enter the festive spirit with a few drinks before opening their deadly gifts from the Count de Bleuchamp, otherwise known as Blofeld. So, to complete our Bondian Christmas, and to provide a suitable period flavour, I've adapted an eggnog recipe dating to 1964,[4] broadly contemporary with the 1969 film.

Serves 2

1 egg
1 tbsp. icing sugar
90 ml. milk
5 tbsp. whisky
5 tbsp. dark rum
⅝ cup/90 ml. double cream
½ tbsp. brandy
Nutmeg

Separate the egg. Put the sugar and yolk into a bowl and whisk together. Stir half the milk into the mixture, add the whisky, mix, then stir in the rum. In another bowl, whisk the egg white until stiff peaks are formed. Add the rest of the milk, cream and brandy to the eggnog mixture, then carefully fold in the white until the mixture is frothy. Spoon the eggnog into glasses, grate a little nutmeg over the top, and serve.

Eggs Gloria

In the film of *On Her Majesty's Secret Service* (1969), Blofeld's right-hand woman Irma Bunt thoughtfully orders steak "Piz Gloria" for James Bond in the revolving restaurant at the Bleuchamp Institute for Allergy Research in Switzerland. The dish comes from the original novel (1963), in which James Bond orders poulet Gloria for dinner from a menu that includes homard Gloria (lobster), tournedos Gloria (beef steak) and other "spécialitiés Gloria". The next day, at lunch, Bond orders oeufs Gloria and a salad, and orders it again before he takes to his skis and escapes Piz Gloria and Blofeld's clutches.[5] But just what is the Glorian style?

The answer: anything covered in a cream and mustard sauce. Poulet Gloria is a spatchcocked chicken covered in a cream and mustard sauce, while the oeufs Gloria are chopped hard-boiled eggs mixed with a cream and cheese sauce, laced with mustard and cooked *au gratin*. Mustard, and English mustard at that, is the defining characteristic; James Bond notes in the book that mustard is typically present in all Glorian dishes. Cheese can be added (ideally a Swiss cheese such as Gruyère), but it's not, it seems, essential.

Here's a recipe for oeufs Gloria, but why stop there? Many more meals can be given a Glorian twist with the addition of a cream and mustard sauce. Why not make a Glorian-style sandwich for lunch? Just add a dollop of sour cream and mustard to your favourite filling.

Serves 2

4 eggs
½ oz./15 g. plain flour
½ oz/15 g. butter
⅜ cup/100 ml. milk
1 oz./25 g. Gruyère cheese, grated
2 tbsp. double cream
2 tsp. English mustard
Black pepper

Boil the eggs for 8 to 10 minutes. Take the saucepan from the heat, cool the eggs with cold water, then remove the shells and slice the eggs.

Put the butter and flour into a saucepan and place on a medium heat. Let the butter melt, using a spatula to combine the butter with the flour, creating a paste. Add the milk and bring to the boil, all the time stirring. As it begins to bubble, the sauce will thicken and become smooth. Mix half of the cheese into the sauce, and, once incorporated, add the cream, mustard, and a pinch of pepper. Cook for a further minute or so.

Remove the saucepan from the heat and add the sliced eggs, mixing well. Spoon the mixture into two ramekins or, better still, tall rings (placed on a baking tray) and pop under a hot grill until the tops are brown and bubbling. Transfer to a plate and serve with a green salad.

Eggs en Cocotte à la Crème

Eggs (or oeufs) en cocotte are baked eggs and, after scrambled, must James Bond's second favourite type of egg dish, given the number of references to the dish in Bond's literary adventures, including shirred eggs in *Live and Let Die* (1954).[6] Indeed, it's possible that he consumes oeufs en cocotte more often than scrambled eggs, since it's revealed in the novel of *On Her Majesty's Secret Service* (1963) that he practically lives on the dish when in England.[7]

The dish makes a very fleeting appearance in the film series, too. *Oeufs cocotte à la crème* is on the menu James Bond (Sean Connery) picks up at the Café Martinique in Nassau in *Thunderball* (1965).

A cocotte, incidentally, is a long-handled ceramic bowl that takes a single egg, but an ordinary ramekin will do just as well for this dish.

Serves 2

Butter for greasing
2 eggs
¼ cup/50 ml. double cream

1 tsp. dried parsley
1 tsp. dried tarragon
Salt and black pepper

Heat the oven to 400°F (200°C/180°C fan-assisted). Grease two ramekins with butter and break one egg into each.

Whisk the cream until soft peaks can be formed. Add the herbs and a pinch or two of salt and pepper to the cream and stir in. Share the cream between both ramekins, covering the eggs.

Cover the ramekins with foil and place them in a shallow baking tray filled with just-boiled water; the water should reach halfway up the sides of the ramekins. Put the pan in the oven and bake for about 15 minutes. The eggs should be served in the ramekins, although I once turned them out onto steaks and the result was delicious.

Fried Eggs

As the Orient Express rattles through Slovenia in *From Russia with Love* (1957), James Bond and Tatiana Romanova sit down in the restaurant car to a breakfast of fried eggs, hard brown bread, and coffee that was mostly chicory.[8]

If this seems like a remarkably rustic and basic meal for the luxury train, it nonetheless reflects the region through which the train is travelling and is in keeping with James Bond's tastes. Eggs for breakfast are, of course, a given. Normally Bond's eggs are scrambled, but occasionally he opts for fried. We don't know how many eggs he orders, but, writing in response to a critic, Ian Fleming claimed that "four fried eggs has [sic] the sound of a real man's meal,"[9] and we can easily imagine that there are four eggs on Bond's plate.

The hard brown bread brings to mind rye bread. It's something of a staple in eastern European countries (and a speciality of the Koroška region of Slovenia), and it's possible that the train picked up supplies during its eight-hour stop in Belgrade. In any case, James Bond is rather partial to rye bread himself, having, for example, poached eggs and rye toast on board the Manta in *Thunderball* (1961) and a slice of pumpernickel in Geneva in *Goldfinger* (1959).[10] The bread that Bond takes on the Orient Express doesn't appear to have been toasted, but I hope at least that it was well buttered.

As for the coffee, chicory is a well-known coffee substitute and historically has been used with coffee or on its own during times of coffee shortages. The comment that Bond's coffee was mostly chicory is likely to allude to the food deprivations that were endemic in the Eastern Bloc. In Britain, the drink is synonymous with Camp coffee, chicory and coffee essence that is stirred into hot milk or used as a flavouring in cakes and desserts.

Poached Eggs/Eggs Benedict

Even James Bond gets nervous. In the novel of *Thunderball* (1961), onboard the Manta submarine with only a few hours to go before the underwater attack on Emilio Largo's Disco, he attempts to eat some poached eggs, only to peck at them and push them away.[11]

Still, James Bond appears to develop a taste for poached eggs after Operation Thunderball. The eggs in "eggs Benedict" are poached, of course, and he eats the dish while in Japan in *You Only Live Twice* (1964) and has them again as a late-night supper in Jamaica in *The Man with the Golden Gun* (1965).[12] Poached eggs are on the menu at the MI6 safehouse at Blayden in the film of *The Living Daylights* (1987): we see a large egg-poacher on the hob during the fistfight between Necros (Andreas Wisniewski) and the butler (Bill Weston).

Typically, eggs Benedict consists of toast or an English muffin topped in sequence with bacon or ham, eggs and hollandaise sauce. For a version worthy of James Bond, the hollandaise must replaced by a mousseline sauce, and the bacon must be smoked bacon.

Serves 2

> **Basic poached eggs:**
> 2 eggs
> Water
> 1–2 tbsp. vinegar
> **Additional ingredients for eggs Benedict:**
> 2 rashers smoked bacon
> 1 muffin (English)
> 1 tsp. parsley, finely chopped
> Mousseline sauce (see page 53)
> Black pepper

If making eggs Benedict, prepare the mousseline sauce in advance. To poach the eggs, fill a large saucepan with water and a splash or two of vinegar and bring the water to the boil. Gently break the eggs into the pan, allowing plenty of space around each egg. (I tend to crack the egg into a small bowl or cup, then tip the egg gently into the saucepan, thus avoiding scalding myself from the steam.) Reduce the heat so that the water is simmering.

Carefully lift the eggs out of the saucepan—ideally using a slotted spoon or pasta scoop—after 2 minutes. Serve on rye toast. If not serving immediately, lower the egg into a bowl of cold water.

For eggs Benedict, fry or grill the bacon. Cut the muffin in half and lightly toast the halves. Place each half on a grill pan or baking tray, place the bacon on top, then balance the poached eggs on top of the bacon. Spoon a generous amount of the sauce on top of the eggs, then sprinkle a pinch of pepper and parsley over the sauce. Pop the grill pan or tray under a hot grill for 2–3 minutes.

Quails' Eggs with Seaweed

Quails' eggs and seaweed, like café complet or figs and yoghurt, is a combination that is mentioned in both the literary and cinematic adventures of James Bond. In the novel of *You Only Live Twice* (1964), James Bond is served lobster, rice, raw quails' egg in sauce and bowls of sliced seaweed at a hostel in the Japanese seaside village of Gamagori.[13] Bond's thoughts about the quails' eggs and seaweed go unrecorded, although in fairness, he's understandably distracted by the lobster's head that crawls off the plate.

In what appears to be a nod to this meal, the manager of Hong Kong's Rubyeon Royale Hotel (Ho Yi) offers James Bond (Pierce Brosnan) lobster, quails' eggs and sliced seaweed in *Die Another Day* (2002).

My recipe is inspired by these two occasions. The dish is quick to prepare, making it a perfect starter or snack.

Serves 2

A dozen quails' eggs
1 tbsp. soy sauce
1 tbsp. mirin
Sprinkling of sugar
1 sheet nori (for sushi)
1 tsp. sesame seeds

Bring a small pan of water to the boil, then carefully place the eggs in the pan. Boil the eggs for 2½ minutes, then drain and cool the eggs under cold water.

Mix the soy sauce, mirin and sugar in a bowl. Peel the eggs, then place the eggs in the bowl, turning them gently to coat them with the sauce.

Finely chop the nori sheet. Heat a small frying pan, then over a medium heat, dry-roast the sesame seeds, cooking them (stirring frequently) for about 2 minutes until they have turned a light brown. Add the chopped seaweed and continue stirring for about 30 seconds.

Tip the sesame seeds and seaweed into the bowl, then gently turn all the ingredients to mix. Serve, ideally with a glass of sake.

Quiche des Cabinet

Quiche des Cabinet, from *A View to a Kill* (1985). Photo: Author

Something's not quite right about the quiche des cabinet (as it's spelt in the script) that James Bond (Roger Moore) cooks in Stacey Sutton's (Tanya Roberts) kitchen in *A View to a Kill* (1985), and it's not just the French grammar. The quiche had clearly been cooked in a flan or quiche tin, but it's not in the tin when Bond pulls it out of the oven. I suspect that the quiche was cooked, removed from the tin, and transferred onto a serving plate before being put back in the oven for the sake of the shot. Either that, or Bond had gone out to buy a quiche from a local delicatessen and pretended he'd made it.

The name of the dish refers to the fact that James has prepared it using random ingredients found in the kitchen cupboards. Stacey mentions that there's not much in the kitchen apart from leftovers in the fridge. These obviously include green and red peppers, and I wouldn't mind betting that there's some ham or bacon in the quiche too. James has also made use of a jar of black olives.

The dish is fairly simple to reconstruct—the hardest aspect is the pastry, but you can always buy ready-made pastry. Next time you watch *A View to a Kill*, have a go at making quiche des cabinet for a more immersive experience.

Serves 4–6

For the pastry:
8 oz./225 g. plain flour
4 oz./115 g. butter
Pinch of salt
2–3 tbsp. cold water
For the filling:
2 oz./50–60 g. diced ham or bacon
½ green pepper, cut into strips
½ red pepper, cut into strips
4 oz./115 g. grated cheese (cheddar or similar)
½ cup/140 ml. milk
½ cup/140 ml. double cream
3 eggs, whisked
1 tsp. finely chopped parsley
Pinch of salt and black pepper
4–5 black olives, pitted and sliced

Start with the pastry. In a mixing bowl, mix the flour and butter together with your fingers until the mixture resembles breadcrumbs. Add the salt, then sprinkle two tablespoons of water evenly over the mixture. Turn the mixture over with a tablespoon or knife, then bring it together with your hands to form a dough. If necessary, add a little more water. Knead the dough until it's smooth. Put the dough into a food bag and refrigerate for about 15 to 20 minutes.

Meanwhile, heat the oven to 400°F (200°C/180°C fan-assisted), then prepare the filling. Put the bacon or ham, green and red peppers, cheese, salt and black pepper, parsley, milk and cream, and whisked eggs into a mixing bowl. Mix all the ingredients together.

Grease a quiche or flan tin with butter. Take the dough out of the fridge. On a lightly flour-dusted surface, roll out the pastry to form a circular shape that's slightly greater in diameter than the tin. Gently roll the pastry around the rolling pin, then lay the pastry over the top of the tin. Press the pastry into the tin (again gently), then cut away the excess pastry from the top of the rim. Prick the base a few times with the points of a fork.

Spoon the filling mixture into the pastry base. Place the sliced olives in the centre. Put the tin in the oven (carefully ensuring that the filling doesn't spill over the edge of the tin; it may be helpful to put the tin on a baking tray) and cook for about 40 minutes. Once cooked—the egg mixture should have risen and be firm to the touch—allow the quiche to rest for a few minutes. Lift the quiche out of the tin and serve. Voilà!

Scrambled Eggs

James Bond consumes scrambled eggs with obsessive regularity throughout his adventures. Breakfast, lunch, or dinner: he eats it anytime and anywhere. The dish is mentioned in almost all the novels and short stories. Only in four novels—*From Russia with Love* (1957), *You Only Live Twice* (1964) and *The Man with the Golden Gun* (1965)—are eggs not scrambled in the line of duty. So frequently were scrambled eggs described in a draft of *Live and Let Die* (1954) that a proof-reader suggested that Bond's addiction was becoming a security risk, obliging Ian Fleming to vary the menus in a subsequent draft.[14]

Bond owes his fondness for the dish entirely to his creator. Ian Fleming acknowledged that his own favourite food was scrambled eggs,[15] and claimed that "scrambled eggs never let you down".[16] Occasionally they did, however: in a letter to his wife Ann Fleming, Ian admitted that he had eaten a breakfast of bad scrambled eggs.[17]

In the short story, "007 in New York", one of James Bond's final adventures, Ian Fleming rewarded Bond with a signature recipe for scrambled eggs. In the tale, while in New York to meet a former Secret Service employee, James Bond recalls how, on a previous visit to the city, he had instructed the kitchen staff of New York's Plaza

Hotel to make the dish just how he likes it. His recipe, "Scrambled eggs 'James Bond'", is given in full as a footnote.[18]

The story first appeared in the *Sunday Herald Tribune* on 29th September 1963, but the recipe had been published before then: in 1961 in a collection of favourite recipes of the famous, *Celebrity Cooking for You*.[19] This earlier version was essentially the same as that which appeared in "007 in New York", but there were slight differences; it stated, for instance, that cream could be used instead of a final piece of butter. However, this was not the first time that the recipe had appeared in print. Onc of Ian Fleming's "Atticus" columns in the *Sunday Times* included a small piece about scrambled eggs under the heading "Oeufs Attique" and attributed the final word on the best scrambled eggs to Mr. Bartolemo Calderoni, the chef of the May Fair hotel in London.[20] Mr. Calderoni's recipe duly appeared below that piece. Again, there are slight differences between this recipe and Fleming's, but much of the recipe is more or less identical to the version published subsequently. Thus, "scrambled eggs 'James Bond'" are really "scrambled eggs 'Bartolemo Calderoni'".

The May Fair Hotel, London, the birthplace of scrambled eggs "James Bond". Photo: Author

Whatever the origin of the recipe, it has two defining qualities. First, it is moist to the point of being undercooked; Ann Fleming described Ian's omelettes as being very "baveuse", literally like drool,[21] and his scrambled eggs were presumably of a similar consistency. Second, with a ratio of one ounce of butter per egg, the dish is extremely buttery. Cooked this way, the eggs are sublime and luxurious. Some of Ian Fleming's other creations thought so too. Sluggsy, one of Vivienne Michel's tormentors in *The Spy Who Loved Me* (1962), likes his scrambled eggs "nice and wet". At Piz Gloria, in *On Her Majesty's Secret Service* (1963), one of the patients receiving Blofeld's special treatment at his allergy clinic asks the waiter Franz for runny scrambled eggs.[22]

If all that whets your appetite, here's a recipe for scrambled eggs adapted from Ian Fleming's instructions.

Serves 2

6 eggs, whisked
3 oz./90 g. salted butter
1–2 tsp. finely chopped herbs (for example, parsley, tarragon, or chives)
A pinch each of salt and black pepper

Melt 2 oz. (60 g) of the butter in a frying pan or saucepan over a medium heat. When the butter begins to bubble, pour in the eggs. Reduce the heat to low, add the salt, pepper and herbs, then turn and scrape the mixture with a spatula or fork, continuing to do so until (and this is the crucial bit) the eggs are reasonably firm but still a little too moist for eating. Take the pan off the heat and stir in the remaining butter, during which time the eggs will have firmed up, although they will remain on the soft side. Serve with hot buttered toast and pink Champagne.

Swiss Cheese Selection

James Bond's final lunch-time meal at Piz Gloria in the novel of *On Her Majesty's Secret Service* (1963) is necessarily on the heavy side: paté maison, followed by oeufs Gloria (eggs smothered in a mustard and cheese sauce), with a cheese tray to finish. Well, James Bond is preparing to make his escape from Blofeld's alpine lair, and so is determined to get a bit of stuffing inside him.[23] That said, we're told that Bond toys with his cheese, so it seems he doesn't have much of an appetite anyway.

What cheeses have been selected for the cheese tray are not specified, but presumably they include some of the famous cheeses of Switzerland. Gruyère and Emmental are probably a given, and there might also be slices of Appenzeller and Raclette.

During a visit to my local supermarket to purchase whatever Swiss cheeses it had on offer, I managed to find Gruyère, Emmental, Fior della Alpi (a cheese made at Schwyz that, so the packaging told me, was "fruity and gently spicy with a subtle crunch and a unique character produced by lush mountain grass and meadow herbs"), and a chunk of Raclette. I was especially pleased to find the Raclette. Although the cheese isn't mentioned in the 1963 novel, it does appear in the 1969 film adaptation. Look closely in the scene where James Bond (George Lazenby) is pursued by Blofeld's goons through the village festival below Piz Gloria, and you'll see a stall selling Raclette. Traditionally, the cut edge of a Raclette wheel is melted and the cheese scraped over potatoes. Whether that's what's on offer on the stall is hard to tell, but it's a possibility.

Incidentally, Gruyère and Emmental are the standard cheeses used in a fondue. There's no evidence in the novels that James Bond ever indulges in a fondue, but the cinematic Bond may have done; there's what looks suspiciously like a fondue set in James Bond's (Roger Moore) kitchen in *Live and Let Die* (1973).

Welsh Rarebit

Posh cheese on toast. It's a candidate for the most un-Bondian dish that James Bond eats. In fairness, given that James Bond had just survived a cliff-fall in the novel of *Moonraker* (1955), everything on the menu was bound to look good.

Having taken a walk along the coast near Dover in Kent and close to Sir Hugo Drax's rocket establishment, James Bond and Special Branch officer Gala Brand are relaxing on the beach, when the white cliffs above them are dynamited and the chalk tumbles all around. Dazed, cut, bruised, and covered in chalk dust, they walk along the shingle to St Margaret's Bay. They clean themselves and take a meal of Welsh rarebit and a few brandies at the Granville Hotel, which is on the top of the cliff overlooking the bay.[24]

Ian Fleming knew the area well. He himself had been a regular visitor to St Margaret's Bay since 1948, when his friend and neighbour in Jamaica, Noël Coward, invited Ian and his future wife Ann Rothermere to use one of the white-painted cottages that he owned at the foot of the white cliffs to escape unwanted attention as they conducted their affair. Ian loved his visits there, and in 1951 gladly took over the lease of one of the cottages when its resident, thriller writer Eric Ambler, decided to move out. Ian called his house "Summer's Lease", and he and Ann would travel down from London over many weekends and summers. The house offered them both a retreat and seclusion, but for Ian the house also provided a convenient base for rounds of golf at Royal St George's in nearby Sandwich, immortalised as Royal St Mark's in *Goldfinger* (1959), access to the sea (he set up a telescope to look out at the passing ships and the distant coast of France), and inspiration for his writing.[25]

The Granville Hotel really did exist, and in order to reach it from the beach, James and Gala would have walked past "Summer's Lease" and climbed a steep set of steps at the foot of the cliff directly below the hotel.

The white-painted cottages at the foot of the chalk cliffs
at St Margaret's Bay, Kent. Photo: Author

Serves 2

½ oz./15 g. plain flour
½ oz./15 g. butter
⅜ cup/100 ml. milk
1 oz./25 g. Cheddar cheese
1½ tbsp. ale
Black pepper
4 slices bread

Turn on the grill. Grate the cheese, then place the butter and flour in a saucepan. Heat, and stir vigorously until the butter melts and the mixture becomes smooth. Pour in the milk, stirring to combine. When the sauce thickens, stir in the cheese and, when melted, add the ale and a pinch of pepper.

Toast one side of the bread and partially toast the other side. Spread the sauce over the partially toasted side and place under the grill until the topping bubbles and begins to brown.

Accompany with a glass of ale.

Western Sandwich

James Bond often has two of something—a double espresso, a double bourbon, a double-0 number. Even his club sandwich, consumed by him in the novel *Thunderball* (1961), is a double-decker.[26] In the novel of *Live and Let Die* (1954), though, he goes one better. Waking at midday in a motel in Tampa Bay (he'd been having a rough time of it, not least discovering that his best friend had been mauled by a shark), Bond orders a triple-decker western sandwich. He thought it was delicious.[27] And no wonder—it's an omelette sandwich. There could be no better sandwich for a man who practically lives on eggs.

Inspired by the fact that for Bond the sandwich is essentially breakfast, my version of the western sandwich (also known as a Denver sandwich) uses English muffins, rather than ordinary bread. It's not a triple-decker, but two sandwiches per person should more than compensate and set one up for the day.

Serves 2

2–3 shallots, peeled and finely chopped
Half a green bell pepper, deseeded and finely chopped
2 oz./50 g. ham, roughly chopped
4 large eggs
½ tsp. mustard powder
½ tsp. finely chopped parsley
Pinch salt and black pepper
4 English muffins
1 tbsp. vegetable oil
Butter

In a deep frying pan, heat the oil over a medium flame, then add the shallots and green pepper, frying the vegetables, stirring frequently, for 3 or 4 minutes until they have softened. While the vegetables are cooking, break the eggs into a bowl and whisk.

Add the ham, salt, black pepper, mustard powder and parsley to the pan, mix, then pour in the eggs. Stir the mixture around to evenly spread the egg and coat the ingredients well, then let the egg cook for a few minutes until it has set on the bottom. If the pan is oven-proof, pop the pan under a hot grill or in a hot oven for about 5 minutes to cook and brown the top of the omelette. Alternatively, use a plate to flip the omelette over and cook the other side in the pan.

Once the omelette is cooked (it should be set all the way through), remove it from the oven or grill and let it rest for a couple of minutes. As it does so, slice each muffin in half and toast. Butter the toasted muffins, cut the omelette into portions and assemble the sandwiches. For a cheffy touch, use a chef's ring to create neat, muffin-sized omelette discs.

3. Fish and Seafood

Ackee and Saltfish

Breakfast for Cayman Islander Quarrel in the novel of *Dr. No* (1958) is ackee and saltfish and a tot of rum. James Bond thinks it's tough stuff to start one's day on, but for Quarrel, it's most refreshing.[1]

Ackee and saltfish (the former being a fruit related to the lychee) is considered a national dish of Jamaica, and not just at breakfast. As with scrambled eggs, the dish serves equally well as a lunchtime or supper meal. So integral is ackee to Jamaican food culture that it got a name-check in "Underneath the Mango Tree", the song that Honey Ryder (Ursula Andress) sings as she makes her famous entrance onto beach in the film of *Dr. No* (1962).

The dish here is inspired by a recipe that appeared in Jamaica's *Daily Gleaner* in 1979.[2]

Serves 2

7 oz./200 g. saltfish
7 oz./200 g. ackee, cooked or tinned and drained
1 onion, peeled and chopped
2 tomatoes, peeled, de-seeded and coarsely chopped
1 bell pepper, chopped
1 glove of garlic, peeled and chopped
1 chilli, de-seeded and chopped
1 tsp. thyme, finely chopped
Black pepper
1 tbsp. vegetable oil
To garnish:
Cucumber, sliced

Iceberg lettuce, shredded

1 or 2 raw tomatoes, sliced

Soak the saltfish in a bowl of water overnight or for 5–6 hours. Drain, then place the fish in a pan, cover with water, bring the water to a boil and, over a medium heat, simmer for 20 minutes. Once the fish is cooked, remove it from the pan and flake it with a fork or with your fingers, discarding any bones. Put the fish to one side.

In a saucepan or a large frying pan, heat the oil and add the onion, bell pepper and the chopped tomatoes. Cook the ingredients, stirring frequently, over a medium heat until they have softened. Add the garlic, chilli, thyme and a generous pinch of black pepper and continue cooking and stirring for another 2 or 3 minutes. Add the fish and ackee to the pan, combine them with the rest of the ingredients and continue cooking until the fish and ackee have been heated through.

Arrange a few slices of tomato and cucumber and some lettuce onto two plates and spoon the ackee and saltfish mixture onto the plates beside the garnish.

Anchovy Paste Sandwich

Patum Peperium or "The Gentleman's Relish", as eaten by
Mrs. Havelock in "For Your Eyes Only" (1960). Photo: Author

The sandwich, that humble lunchtime staple, appears with surprising frequency in the James Bond adventures. Take the short story "For Your Eyes Only" (1960), in which two types of sandwich are consumed. At one point, outside Montreal, James Bond makes himself some smoked ham sandwiches, while earlier in the story, Mrs. Havelock, whose cruel murder is avenged by her daughter Judy, takes a Patum Peperium sandwich. Patum Peperium, or "The Gentleman's Relish", is anchovy paste. You can still buy it today, but homemade anchovy paste is otherwise quick and simple to prepare.[3]

Makes several sandwiches

2 oz./50 g. drained anchovy fillets
1 tbsp. breadcrumbs
1 tbsp. milk
1 tbsp. olive oil
Pinch of pepper
Slices of bread
Cucumber
Butter (optional)

Crush the anchovy fillets using a pestle and mortar or with a fork. Add the breadcrumbs, olive oil, milk and pepper and mix well until you have a smooth paste. You're now ready to assemble your sandwich. In keeping with the genteel environment of "Content", the Havelocks' Jamaican home, I recommend cutting the crusts off the bread. I also suggest the addition of cucumber (peeled, of course) to balance the saltiness of the paste, which should be applied thinly.

Bouillabaisse

After arriving at Marseille airport during the events of the novel of *On Her Majesty's Secret Service* (1963), James Bond takes a taxi into the city. He strikes up a conversation with his driver, Marius, and the two get on well. Approaching the Vieux Port (Old Port), Bond asks whether the bouillabaisse chez Guido is always as good. Marius replies that it is passable, though laments that true bouillabaisse, which must include scorpion fish, rather than cod, is no more.[4]

Clearly James Bond is familiar with Marseille and its restaurants (or one, at least) and is partial to the city's signature dish, bouillabaisse, or fish stew. Guido itself was a real restaurant and was situated in the Vieux Port on the Quai de Rive Neuve. The Michelin Guide described Guido as a "restaurant élégant", whose speciality was "bouillabaisse des pêcheurs à la rouille". The restaurant was also known for its crayfish and beef, and among its wines were Cassis and Château-Minuty.[5]

Ian Fleming may well have frequented the restaurant himself. He himself visited Marseille in 1953 to report on Jacques Cousteau's underwater excavation of two superimposed ancient wrecks, and indeed in one of his subsequent articles for the *Sunday Times*, Fleming wrote of the harbour restaurants in the Vieux Port.[6]

The choice of fish is considered to be critical. Ian Fleming told his *Sunday Times* readers that the basis of bouillabaisse was scorpion fish and conger eel. Chefs at Marseille's Restaurant Isnard opted for monkfish, scorpion fish, John Dory, whiting, and lobster, as well as scorpion fish and conger eel, or at least they did in the 1950s. The director of the Buffet de Marseille liked to add gurnard.[7] Practically speaking, however, the choice of fish depends on what's on offer at the fishmonger's; I'd happily use cod, huss, sea bass, or sea bream or whatever's going. The most crucial point is that the fish must be fresh.

Serves 4

4 lb./2 kg. assorted fish, skinned, filleted and cut into large chunks
1 lobster, cooked and chopped into portions (retaining the shell)
1 large onion, peeled and chopped

2–3 cloves of garlic, peeled and chopped
2 large tomatoes, peeled and coarsely chopped
⅝ cup/100 ml. dry white wine
1 tbsp. parsley, plus a little more to garnish, coarsely chopped
1 tbsp. thyme, chopped
Pinch saffron
Salt and black pepper
Olive oil
1 baguette
For the stock:
Bones, skins and heads from the filleted fish
1 litre water
1 tsp. peppercorns
1 onion
1 stick of celery
1 bay leaf
1 or 2 sprigs of parsley and thyme

To make the stock, place all the stock ingredients in a saucepan and pour in the water. Bring the liquid to the boil, then simmer rapidly for 20 minutes. Drain the liquid into a bowl or jug.

For the soup, heat a good glug of olive oil in a large saucepan over a moderate heat. Add the tomatoes, onions, and garlic, and gently cook them until soft. Add the wine. While the wine is bubbling away, add the herbs, the saffron and fish. Stir, then add enough stock to cover all the ingredients. Mix well, bring the liquid to the boil, then reduce the heat slightly to achieve a fierce simmer. Cook for 15 minutes.

While the stew is cooking, slice the baguette, brush both sides of each slice with olive oil and toast under the grill.

Remove the soup from the heat. To serve an individual portion, place two of the baguette toasts in a wide bowl, ladle the stew over them, and garnish with pieces of lobster and a sprinkling of parsley.

Bourdeto

Bourdeto, as eaten by James Bond in the film of
For Your Eyes Only (1981). Photo: Author

We are treated to the rare sight of James Bond (Roger Moore) ordering dinner on screen in *For Your Eyes Only* (1981). Dining with Kristatos (Julian Glover) at the casino in Corfu, he orders Preveza prawns, savara salad and bourdeto.

As is often the case in the books, Bond "eats local", bourdeto being a speciality of the island. There are many variations of the dish, but in essence it is fish cooked in a spicy sauce. Traditionally, scorpion fish is used (as it is for another Bondian dish, bouillabaisse), but if unavailable may be substituted with a variety of other fish. For the recipe below, I've used sea bass.

The question of whether or not tomatoes are included in the dish is a matter of debate, with some contending that bourdeto isn't true bourdeto with them. In the spirit of compromise, I've left out the tomatoes, except for a dollop of tomato purée to enhance the dish's flavours and colour.

Serves 2

1–2 whole fish, depending on size (if using sea bass, cook one fish per person), cleaned and with heads and tails removed

1 tbsp. olive oil

1 large onion, peeled and sliced thinly into rings

1–2 cloves garlic, peeled and chopped

2 tsp. paprika

½ tsp. cayenne pepper

1 tbsp. tomato purée

1¾ cups/400 ml. freshly boiled water

Juice of half a lemon

1 tsp. finely chopped parsley

1 tsp. finely chopped oregano

1 tsp. finely chopped red chillies

Pinch each of salt and black pepper

2 lemon wedges

Heat the oven to 400°F (200°C/180°C fan-assisted). In a deep, oven-proof frying pan, heat the olive oil over a medium flame. Fry the onion and garlic until they soften. Add the paprika and cayenne pepper and stir to combine with the onions. Add half the water, tomato purée and the salt and pepper, mix well and allow the sauce to simmer for 3–4 minutes until it is almost dry, the liquid having reduced by about three quarters.

Stir in the remaining water and the lemon juice. Lay the fish in the pan, coating the fish with the sauce and onions. Sprinkle the parsley, oregano, and chilli over the fish. Place the pan uncovered in the oven. (If the pan isn't oven-proof, transfer the sauce and fish to an oven dish.) Cook for 20 minutes.

Remove the pan or dish from the oven. Garnish with lemon wedges and serve with fried potatoes, rice or crusty bread.

Caviar

Caviar, the staple food of the cinematic
James Bond. Photo: Clare McIntyre

Like scrambled eggs, caviar is synonymous with James Bond. More so, in fact. Not only does it appear regularly throughout his literary adventures, but it is also one of the few foods from the books transferred to the big screen, becoming an essential part of the cinematic Bond's identity. Who could forget Daniel Craig's James Bond tucking into caviar and toast with almost a complete lack of ceremony after defeating Le Chiffre at Texas Hold'em in *Casino Royale* (2006)? Here's a man well-used to the finer things in life.

If you want to eat like James Bond, then caviar from the Caspian Sea is a must. There are various types of caviar, but that from the beluga sturgeon is regarded as the best and is naturally the most expensive. Caviar from the oscietra and sevruga sturgeons enjoy lower prices, but if even these are a little out of reach, then salted herring roe and lumpfish roe make good, economical alternatives.

James Bond, of course, eats beluga caviar, as we discover in the film of *On Her Majesty's Secret Service* (1969), when Bond (George Lazenby) dollops a spoonful of caviar on a piece of toast as a sort of post-brawl snack. In the novel of *Thunderball* (1961), Bond (Sean Connery) orders fifty US dollars' worth of the stuff. In today's money, that's about $430, which will buy you a 125-gram or 4-ounce tin of beluga caviar. As an indicator of how much Bond spends on caviar, a menu dating to 1961 from New York's Waldorf Astoria offered "caviar aux blinis" as a starter for a mere $6.50.

Whatever caviar you choose, purchase enough to provide more than a single spoonful per person, and serve it with plenty of hot toast; as Bond says in the novel of *Casino Royale* (1953), the problem is getting enough toast to go with the caviar. We don't know whether Bond prefers his toast buttered, but M takes buttered toast with his caviar in the novel of *Moonraker* (1955).[8] As for accompaniments, Christmas Jones (Denise Richards) in *The World Is Not Enough* (1999) likes sour cream with her caviar, but Bond, according to the novel of *Casino Royale*, prefers chopped onion and an egg, and it's Bond's choice that I give in the preparation below.

Serves 2

4 oz./100–125 g. caviar
4 slices bread
2 eggs
2 shallots
Lemon to garnish

Boil the eggs for 8–10 minutes. Cool the eggs, shell them, then cut them in half and remove the yolks. Finely chop the whites, then the yolks and set them aside. Peel the shallots and finely chop them. Put the shallots, egg white and egg yolk into ramekins or small bowls. Toast the bread and cut into batons or "soldiers".

Spoon the caviar into a bowl and serve along with the accompaniments. Garnish with slices of lemon.

Conch Chowder

James Bond knows a thing or two about conchs. For one thing, they're reputed to be an aphrodisiac. For another, island people have conch chowder on their wedding night. Bond tells Domino Vitali as much while flirting with her over drinks in the Bahamian capital of Nassau in the novel of *Thunderball* (1961).[9] Conch chowder also has the rare distinction of a food that is mentioned both in the original novel and its screen adaptation. My recipe is inspired by one published in Jamaica's *Sunday Gleaner Magazine* in 1968, which in turn was, appropriately, based on a recipe that originated in the Bahamas and is almost certainly contemporary with the novel.[10]

Serves 2

7 oz./200 g. conch meat, cooked (or cooked whelk meat if conchs are unavailable)

Juice of one lime

1 onion, peeled and finely chopped

½ green pepper, deseeded and finely chopped

2 oz./50 g. smoked bacon lardons

2 medium potatoes or 1 large one, peeled and finely diced

1 x 14 oz. (400 g) can chopped tomatoes

2 cups/500 ml. water

2–3 drops hot pepper sauce (or to taste)

Black pepper

1 bay leaf

1 tsp. finely chopped thyme
Butter for frying
Chopped parsley to garnish

Finely chop the conch (or whelk) meat in a food processor, adding the lime juice before processing. (If you don't have a processor, chop the meat by hand and mix it with the lime juice in a bowl.) In a large saucepan, melt the butter over a medium heat. When the butter starts to sizzle, add the onion, green pepper, potato, and lardons. Fry, stirring occasionally, until the onion and pepper soften. Mix in the conch meat, then add the tomatoes, water, bay leaf and thyme. Stir to combine the ingredients, then add the hot pepper sauce and a generous pinch of black pepper. Stir again, then cover the pan and bring the liquid to a boil. Remove the lid, reduce the heat, and allow the chowder to simmer, stirring occasionally, until the potatoes have started to disintegrate, and the chowder is nice and thick (approximately 25–30 minutes). Transfer the chowder to a serving bowl and garnish with a sprinkle of parsley.

Crabmeat Ravigotte

Tiffany Case gives James Bond's suggestion of shellfish and Hock, reputedly a combination with aphrodisiacal properties, short shrift at the "21" Club in the novel of *Diamonds Are Forever* (1956). She tells him that it would take more than crabmeat ravigotte to get her into bed with him.[11] Ravigotte (more usually ravigote) is a vinaigrette-based sauce. As Tiffany Case's remark implies, crabmeat ravigotte would have been regarded as a sophisticated dish at the time that Ian Fleming was writing. It graced the menus of top hotels and restaurants, among them the Waldorf Astoria in New York (a 1953 menu prices the dish at $1.85) and the St. Regis Hotel, also in New York and Bond's hotel in *Live and Let Die*.[12]

Serves 2

7 oz./200 g. crabmeat (drained, if tinned)
For the sauce:
4 tbsp. olive oil
1 tsp. white wine vinegar
2–3 drops lemon juice
1 tsp. shallot, finely chopped
1 tsp. parsley, finely chopped
1 tsp. tarragon, finely chopped
1 tsp. chives, finely chopped
1 tsp. gherkin, finely chopped
1 tsp. capers, finely chopped
1 tsp. Dijon mustard
A pinch of black pepper

Put all the ingredients for the sauce in a bowl and whisk or stir until they are well combined and the sauce thick and creamy. Fold in the crabmeat, making sure that the meat is well coated. Serve with lettuce for a crab cocktail, or, better still, fill a cleaned crab shell with the mixture.

Gratin de Langouste

James Bond's mind does occasionally wander during his pursuit of Goldfinger through France in Ian Fleming's 1959 novel. A daydream of gratin de langouste (lobster gratin) is prompted by the flash of a Triumph and its pretty driver (Tilly Masterton) who overtakes his Aston Martin DB Mark III. James Bond allows himself to imagine a romantic dinner with the driver, the meal comprising gratin de langouste at L'Oustau de la Baumanière on the edge of the village of Les Baux in Province,[13] a luxury restaurant and one of the best tables in France, according to the Michelin Guide. In 1958, the year *Goldfinger* was written, the restaurant's proprietor and chef was

Monsieur Thuilier, whose specialities included fillets of sole with lobster sauce, and leg of lamb en croute.[14]

I don't pretend to be in Monsieur Thuilier's class, but the recipe below, which uses the classic white or Béchamel sauce with a cheese topping, is a tasty enough rendition of this sophisticated French dish.

Serves 2

> 2 lobster tails, cooked
> **For the sauce:**
> ½ oz./15 g. plain flour
> ½ oz./15 g. butter
> ⅜ cup 100 ml. milk
> 1 oz./25 g. Gruyère, grated
> Black pepper

Heat the oven to 390°F (200°C; 180°C fan-assisted). Carefully remove the meat from the tails and slice. Put the flour and the butter in a saucepan and combine over a gentle heat, stirring continuously to create a smooth mixture. Add the milk and a pinch of pepper, stirring until the sauce bubbles and thickens. Take the sauce off the heat.

In a bowl, coat the lobster meat with the sauce. Return the meat to the shells (or arrange in ramekins or small oven dishes) and spoon any leftover sauce over the meat. Sprinkle the cheese over the top, dot with butter and place the lobsters under in the oven for 10–15 minutes or until the cheese has melted and the top is golden brown.

Herrings with Onions in a Cream Sauce

How does James Bond kill time in Berlin before attempting to kill a KGB sniper? In the short story "The Living Daylights" (1966), we find out. He lunches on scrambled eggs (what else?), visits the zoo and other sights of Berlin, and then, feeling rather peckish, has a late afternoon meal of matjes herrings (juvenile herrings preserved in salt) smothered in cream and onion rings.[15] Though matjes herrings are of Dutch origin, Bond has done well to choose herrings in Berlin. In a near-contemporary book of German cooking, it was claimed that "herrings probably get the finest treatment in the world in Germany." [16]

Serves 2

    4 matjes herring fillets
    1 onion, peeled and sliced into rings
    2 tbsp. white wine
    2–4 oz./60–100 g. samphire
    ⅜ cup/100 ml. double cream
    Black pepper
    Oil for frying, approx. 1–2 tbsp.
    Flour for dusting

Heat the oil in a frying pan over a medium heat. Dust the fillets with some flour, then lay them in the pan. Fry for 2 to 3 minutes, then turn the fillets over. Fry for another 2 minutes.

While the fillets are cooking, heat a knob of butter or a little oil in another frying pan, and stir fry the samphire for 1–2 minutes until it has wilted. Take the pan off the heat and put to one side.

Once cooked, transfer the fish fillets to a plate and keep warm. Put the onion rings into the pan and fry gently for 3 to 4 minutes over a medium heat. When they begin to soften, add the wine and continue to cook, reducing the liquid almost completely.

Taking the pan off the heat, pour in the cream and stir to combine with the onion rings and wine. Return the pan to a medium heat and allow the sauce to warm through. Season with a pinch of black pepper. When the cream begins to bubble, remove the pan from the heat.

To serve the herrings (two fillets per person), spoon the sauce generously around the fish and top with a dollop of the samphire.

Littleneck Clams

James Bond begins his meal at Ma Frazier's in Harlem during the events of the novel of *Live and Let Die* (1954) with some littleneck clams.[17] As with any type of clam, littlenecks can be prepared in a variety of ways. For me, though, clams are best cooked simply with few ingredients. Here, then, is a basic but very tasty recipe for steamed clams.

Serves 2

> 2 dozen littleneck clams
> 100 ml. dry white wine
> 2 tbsp. parsley, chopped
> Black pepper
> 2 lemon wedges

Rinse the clams, discarding any that fail to close after handling or a gentle tap. Pour the wine into a large saucepan. Tip in the clams, add the parsley and a pinch of pepper. Cover the saucepan with a lid and put the pan over a high heat. The wine should rapidly come to a boil, filling the saucepan with steam. The clams should open in no more than 4 or 5 minutes. If the clams have not opened in that time, give the pan a shake and continue cooking for another minute or two. Spoon the clams into bowls and squeeze the juice from the lemon wedges over the clams. Serve with bread and butter.

Lobster Salad

Lobster salad is among the lunchtime buffet dishes about which James Bond fantasises while pursuing Scaramanga through a mangrove swamp in Jamaica in the novel of *The Man with the Golden Gun* (1965).[18] Lunch had been promised by Scaramanga following a train ride, which had terminated sooner than expected. If the food had actually been served, the lobster salad may have looked something like this recipe, which is inspired by an advertisement for the "Bird in Hand" restaurant in Jamaica's *Daily Gleaner* in 1964.[19]

Serves 2

The meat, cut into chunks, from 1 or 2 cooked lobsters
¼ iceberg lettuce, shredded
1 stick of celery, sliced
1 tomato, cut into thin wedges
1 tsp. chopped capers
Flesh from 1 avocado, cut into chunks
2 hard-boiled eggs, peeled and sliced
For the dressing:
1 tbsp. lime juice
1 tbsp. olive oil
1 tsp. white wine vinegar
1 tsp. finely chopped red chilli
Salt and black pepper

Throw all the salad ingredients into a bowl. Combine the dressing ingredients in another, smaller bowl, adding a pinch each of salt and black pepper. Pour the dressing into the salad bowl and toss the salad. Serve the salad with crusty bread or french fries.

Lobster Tails, Broiled

Lobster, caviar and Champagne: food and
drink fit for James Bond. Photo: Clare Abbott

When I opportunistically bought two lobster tails from my local supermarket, I didn't have a recipe in mind, but it didn't take long before inspiration struck. In this case, I turned to the novel of *Dr. No* (1958). In the book, James Bond and his ally in Jamaica, Quarrel, scan the menu of "The Joy Boat" restaurant in Kingston harbour and decide on broiled lobster and rare steak with native vegetables.[20] Presumably, James and Quarrel enjoy whole lobster, but lobster tails are a more economical option. What's more, they're quick to prepare and cook and look just as good.

This recipe has been adapted from a recipe for broiled lobster that appeared in the *Sunday Gleaner* in 1957,[21] published shortly after Ian Fleming had returned to London from Jamaica carrying the first draft of *Dr. No*.

Serves 2

2 lobster tails, uncooked
Melted butter

Paprika
Parsley, finely chopped

Switch on the grill or, if preferred, heat the oven to 390°F (200°C; 180°C fan-assisted).

Take one of the tails and with sharp scissors or kitchen shears make a cut lengthwise down the middle of the shell, stopping when you reach the tail fins. Don't worry if you cut into the flesh a little. Carefully run a finger between the shell and the meat and around the top end of the tail to loosen the meat. Gently pull the meat up so that it is raised above the shell (ensuring that the meat is still attached to the fin end). Remove the digestive tract. Repeat with the other lobster tail.

If using the grill, place the tails meat-side down on a baking tray. Grill for 2 or 3 minutes, then turn the tails over so that the meat is facing the grill. Before popping the tails back under the grill, brush the meat liberally with melted butter and sprinkle some paprika and parsley over the tails. Continue cooking, allowing a total cooking time of 10–15 minutes.

If using the oven, place the tails meat-side up on a baking tray. Brush with melted butter and add paprika and parsley. Put the tray in the oven and cook the tails for 10–15 minutes.

Make sure the meat is sizzling and cooked through before serving. If not (and larger lobster tails may need longer cooking), put them back under the heat for another couple of minutes.

Octopus Stew

Poor Octopussy. First, Major Dexter Smythe force-feeds it a deadly scorpion fish just to see how it would fare, then two fishermen kill it with the major's spear and have it for supper.[22] What an ignoble end for the creature of the eponymous short story published in book form in 1966.

At least it died for a good cause. How did the fishermen cook it? We aren't told, but I've got an idea that, benefitting from slow cooking, the octopus was stewed. Here's one method inspired by Jamaican recipes.

Serves 2

Approx. 17½ oz./500 g. octopus, cleaned and chopped into bite-sized pieces
Juice from 1 lime
1 tbsp. vegetable oil
1 large tomato, finely chopped
1 red pepper, chopped
1–2 cloves garlic, finely chopped
1 tsp. thyme, finely chopped
1 tsp. (or to taste) hot pepper sauce
Dash or two soy sauce
Pinch each salt and black pepper
1 cup/250 ml. coconut milk
Finely chopped parsley to garnish

In a bowl, combine the octopus and lime juice and allow the octopus to marinate for at least an hour or preferably overnight.

Tip the contents of the bowl into a flame-proof casserole or saucepan and cover with a lid. Over a very low heat, allow the octopus to cook in its own juices for about 20 minutes, stirring very occasionally.

In the meantime, heat the oil in a frying pan over a medium heat and gently cook the tomato and red pepper until softened. Add the garlic, thyme, hot pepper sauce, soy sauce and salt and black pepper, and mix well. Transfer the contents of the frying pan to the casserole, then pour in the coconut milk. Stir thoroughly, bring the liquid to the boil, replace the lid, then allow the stew to simmer for 50 minutes to an hour, stirring occasionally.

Serve the stew with Jamaican-style rice and peas and garnish with parsley.

Oyster Stew

Oyster Bar, Grand Central Station, the best place for oyster stew
in New York, according to Ian Fleming. Photo: Author

As James Bond reflects in the short story "007 in New York" (1963),
lunchtime in the city is not like the old days. Now, in Bond's view,
the restaurants and bars are filled with businessmen with expense
accounts, resulting in inflated prices and bad food. Bond can rely,
however, on the Oyster Bar in Grand Central Station, which serves,
in Bond's view, the best meal in New York: oyster stew.[23] This was
one of Ian Fleming's favourite haunts, too, and he gave Bond his
fondness for the dish.[24]

My version of this creamy stew is quick to prepare. If you're
unable to find fresh oysters, then smoked oysters make an equally
delicious alternative. Traditionally, small, button-like crackers accompany the stew, but freshly made croutons can be used
instead.

Serves 2

Generous knob of butter for frying
1 medium stick of celery, finely sliced

1 medium onion (or 2–3 shallots), peeled and finely chopped
⅝ cup/150 ml. milk (semi-skimmed is fine)
⅝ cup/150 ml. double cream
A dozen fresh oysters
Pinch black pepper
1 tsp. smoked paprika
2–3 splashes Worcestershire sauce
1 tsp. finely chopped parsley

Shuck the oysters and remove the meat from the shell. Place the meat, along with the liquor, into a bowl.

Melt the butter in a saucepan over a medium heat. Add the onion and celery and cook, stirring frequently, for approximately 5 minutes until the vegetables have softened. Pour in the milk and cream and bring to the boil. Tip in the oysters and the liquor and add the paprika, black pepper and Worcestershire sauce. Stir, then bring the stew to the boil. Allow the stew to boil for half a minute or so. Ladle the stew into bowls and sprinkle the parsley over the top. If available, accompany with oyster crackers and a Miller High Life beer.

Oysters with Tabasco Sauce

There's no doubt about it: Tabasco Brand Pepper Sauce is the sauce of Bond villains. Scaramanga (Christopher Lee) tells Nick Nack (Hervé Villechaize) to fetch a bottle at the very beginning of 1974's *The Man with the Golden Gun* ("Nick Nack! Tabasco!"), while in *The Spy Who Loved Me* (1977), a bottle can be seen on Karl Stomberg's (Curd Jürgens) dining table in his underwater base, Atlantis.

Both villains use the sauce to spice up their oysters. Preparing oysters à la Stromberg (or Scaramanga) is simplicity itself; the addition of just a drop of Tabasco sauce is a taste sensation and positively wicked.

Serves 2

A dozen oysters
Wedges cut from half a lemon
Bottle of Tabasco sauce

Pile some crushed ice on a serving plate or platter. Shuck the oysters, taking care not to spill the liquor, and place the half-shells on the ice. Arrange the lemon wedges artfully on the platter and serve. Just before you tuck into each oyster, add a drop or two of lemon juice and Tabasco sauce. Enjoy!

Poached Turbot with Mousseline Sauce

Recounting his drive through France early in the novel of *On Her Majesty's Secret Service* (1963), James Bond admits that he had had his fill of French tourist-centred cuisine and the "spécialités du chef" and other bloated epithets attached to inferior sauces and poor-quality meats, and of the self-satisfied rituals that form the tenets of the religions of food and wine. A bad meal on the bank of the Loire was the final straw, obliging Bond to revert to the tried and tested, ringing up his old friend Monsieur Bécaud, proprietor of a modest restaurant exactly opposite the railway station of Étaples in northern France, to book a table. Two hours later, Bond leaves the establishment having enjoyed a dinner of poached turbot with sauce mousseline and half a roast partridge.[25]

At the time of James Bond's adventure, there were two restaurants opposite the railway station: the Hotel des Voyageurs and the Normandie.[26] Of the two, the Voyageurs is nearer the station's ticket office and therefore closer to being exactly opposite the station. The Normandie has long since closed down, but the Voyageurs still exists. Being a large hotel, bar and brasserie on the corner of the street, the latter doesn't quite accord with Fleming's modest establishment, and it may be that he meant the Normandie. However, the Michelin Guide categorised the Voyageurs as a very plain, but adequate hotel, so perhaps the restaurant was modest enough.

The Voyageurs in Étaples, France, a strong candidate for the restaurant visited by James Bond in *On Her Majesty's Secret Service* (1963). Photo: Author

Not so long ago, I had the opportunity to visit the restaurant (alas, poached turbot was off the menu). The elderly woman who served me told me that she had worked at the Voyageurs for thirty-odd years. She showed me some vintage photographs of the establishment—the hotel appeared to have been long past its glory days—but she wasn't familiar with the name of Monsieur Bécaud.

Returning to Bond, what could be a better way to restore faith in the local cuisine than poached turbot? This is a large flat fish; a starter for two people should require no more than a fillet. The mousseline sauce is close to a hollandaise sauce, but with whipped cream added at the end. You needn't confine its preparation to turbot; James Bond also has it with asparagus in the novel of *Diamonds Are Forever* (1956).[27]

There are many variations of the sauce, but I've taken my cue from a recipe devised by chef and hotel proprietor Monsieur Pic, first published in 1952.[28]

Serves 2

2 pieces of turbot fillet
Fish stock or water
1 tsp. peppercorns
1 bay leaf
1 sprig parsley
Lemon juice
For the sauce:
1 tsp. lemon juice
1 tsp. cold water
2 egg yolks
1½ oz./30 g. butter
Pinch of salt and black pepper
2 tbsp. double cream, whisked to soft peaks

Place the fillet pieces in a wide, shallow saucepan or deep frying pan, add the herbs, peppercorns and a few drops of lemon juice, and cover with the stock or water. Bring to a gentle simmer and cook for 10 minutes. Transfer the fish to a plate and keep warm.

Make the sauce as the fish is cooking. Quarter-fill a small saucepan with water, place it over a medium heat and bring the water to the boil. Reduce to a very low heat, so that steam, rather than bubbles, emanates from the water.

Fill a bowl or small basin with the teaspoon of water, the lemon juice, a pinch or two of pepper, a small piece of butter, and the egg yolks. Sit the basin on top of the saucepan and whisk the ingredients to create a smooth mixture, taking care not to allow the water to come to a simmer.

Add the remaining butter bit by bit, whisking each small portion fully into the sauce before adding another knob. Once all the butter has been incorporated, continue to whisk until the sauce has thickened to soft peaks. This will take a good ten minutes of whisking, so be patient. Take the bowl off the heat, then fold in the cream. Serve the fish, spooning the sauce generously over the pieces.

Quenelles de Brochet

Entering Orléans during his pursuit of Goldfinger through France in Ian Fleming's 1959 novel, James Bond reflects that in other circumstances he would have spent a night at the Auberge de la Montespan, situated on the north bank of the Loire two kilometres south-west of the city centre on the N152 (now the D2152), his belly full of quenelles de brochet.

As with many of the places in the Bond novels, the Auberge de la Montespan really existed. At the time that Fleming wrote *Goldfinger*, the establishment, according to the Michelin Guide, offered a very comfortable restaurant and rooms equipped with all mod-cons: central heating, a private bath, and—quel luxe!—a bidet with running water.[29]

If time and weather permitted, James Bond would have taken his meals at a table on the auberge's magnificent terrace overlooking the river and perhaps, if he were lucky, caught a game or two of tennis at one of the many tennis tournaments that the auberge hosted. He may have chatted with the proprietor, Monsieur Fournier, whose son was the head chef.[30]

The former chateau, which famously hosted a visit from the French king, Louis XIV, in 1685, is, so far as I know, closed to visitors, but it can be seen from the street, being located on the south side of the road from Orléans to Blois between Rue de Maison Rouge and Rue du Clos de la Montespan.

As for the quenelles de brochet, these are mousse-like fish dumplings made with pike. Traditionally, the mixture before cooking is refined by pressing it through sieves, but these days the food processor does the job equally well. If pike is hard to come by or prohibitively expensive, then any white, flaky fish, such as cod or haddock, makes a good alternative.

Serves 2

Approx. 11 oz./300 g. (a little more or less is fine) pike fillet, skinned and boned

1 egg white

¼ cup/40 ml. double cream

Pinch each of salt and pepper

1 tsp. parsley

1 tsp. dill

3 pints/1½ litres fish or vegetable stock

For the sauce:

½ oz./15 g. plain flour

½ oz./15 g. butter

⅜ cup/100 ml. milk

2 tbsp. double cream

1 tsp. finely chopped parsley

1 tsp. finely chopped dill

Coarsely chop the fish, place it in a food processor, add the remaining items except the stock and blend for 20–30 seconds or so until you have a smooth-ish paste. Refrigerate the mixture for at least 1 hour.

When ready to cook, bring the stock to a boil in a large saucepan over a high heat. Reduce the heat right down to its lowest setting so that the stock is very barely simmering—the occasional small bubble rising to the top should be the only clue that there is still heat below the pan.

Take a tablespoon of fish mixture and, with a second tablespoon, mould the mixture into an egg shape. You will probably need to pass the dumpling from one spoon to the other a few times to achieve a firm, smooth shape. (I haven't tried it, but I imagine an ice-cream scoop would work well, although the dumplings will of course be round, rather than oval.) Gently drop the dumpling into the saucepan and repeat with the remaining mixture. You should be able to make 6–8 dumplings. Poach the dumplings for 8–10 minutes. As they cook, they will rise to the surface.

While they're cooking, prepare a quick dill and parsley sauce. In a small saucepan, combine the flour and butter over a medium heat. When you have a smooth mixture, add the milk and stir until you have a thick sauce that is beginning to bubble. Stir in the cream, parsley and dill. (If the sauce is a little too thick—it should coat the back of a spoon but be thin enough to pour—add a little more milk or water.)

Divide the dumplings between two plates and cover liberally with the sauce.

Raie au Beurre Noir

The stingray in the short story "The Hildebrand Rarity" (1960) is James Bond's Moby Dick. True, the fish hasn't taken his leg or even stung him, but Bond has an obsession about pursuing and killing the ray that Captain Ahab would recognise. James Bond succeeds—Ian Fleming's description of the struggle between man and fish is as evocative as anything in Herman Melville's great American novel—and suggests to his Seychellois host Fidele Barbey the classic dish of raie au beurre noir: ray wing with black butter.[31]

Fleming recounts that in times gone by, the tail of the stingray was used as a whip. The detail was not lost on the writers of Licence to Kill (1989), Richard Maibaum and Michael G. Wilson, who placed such an item in the hands of drug-lord Franz Sanchez (Robert Davi).

Raie au beurre noir, a meal suggestion for Bond made in
"The Hildebrand Rarity" (1960). Photo: Clare McIntyre

Serves 2

2 skate wings
Fish stock or water
1 tsp. peppercorns
1 bay leaf
1 tbsp. parsley
1 tsp. tarragon
For the sauce:
2 oz./50 g. butter
1 tbsp. white wine vinegar
1 tbsp. lemon juice
1 tbsp. capers
1 tbsp. parsley
Salt and black pepper

Place the skate wings in a large pan or deep frying pan along with the herbs, peppercorns and some lemon juice and cover with stock or water. If the fish are too large for a single pan, cook separately or use two pans. Bring the water to a simmer and poach the fish for 10–15 minutes. Transfer the fish to plates and keep warm.

Heat the butter, vinegar and lemon juice in a saucepan over a high heat. Cook until the butter has melted and is sizzling and takes on a dark brown colour. In the meantime, chop the parsley and capers.

Remove the pan from the heat, season the butter and add the parsley and capers. Pour the sauce over the wings

Salmon Fillets

In the film of *Goldfinger* (1964), James Bond (Sean Connery) and Goldfinger's moll, Jill Masterson (Shirley Eaton), enjoy an evening together in James's suite at the Fontainebleau in Miami. Naturally, a feast for the taste buds, as well as the eyes, is provided. Accompanying the inevitable Champagne is a platter of salmon fillets, asparagus tips, cucumber slices, red peppers stuffed with peas, and lettuce. There's also an hors d'oeuvres dish with more asparagus, tomatoes and what appears to be potato salad. A bowl of fruit comprising, among other items, pears, grapes, apples, possibly a plum, a banana and, oddly enough, a cucumber, can be seen behind the tray.

Here I'm concentrating on the salmon fillets, and for this dish, the salmon is cooked "en papillote": the fillets are wrapped in greaseproof paper and cooked in the oven. It's an efficient method: a little steam is created within the parcel, reducing the cooking time and preventing the food from drying out.

Serves two

2 salmon fillets
Black pepper

Lemon juice

Salt

To garnish:

3–4 slices of cucumber per fillet

2 pimento slices

Heat the oven to 375°F 190°C (170°C fan-assisted). Place the salmon on a large piece of greaseproof or baking paper. Sprinkle a little salt and black pepper and a few drops of lemon juice over the fish. Wrap the fish loosely in the paper, transfer the "package" to a baking tray and place the tray in the oven for approximately 20 minutes.

Once cooked, place the fish onto plates and garnish with the cucumber and pimento slices.

Sardines en Papillote

Darko Kerim Bey, James Bond's Turkish host in the novel of *From Russia with Love* (1957), is keen for Bond to try a few sardines grilled en papillote. James Bond isn't overly impressed, claiming that the sardines tasted like any other fried sardines,[32] but I wonder whether they were cooked correctly. We'll never know, but I've found that the dish is well worth the effort.

Usually, the food is cooked in the oven, but for the authentic Bond experience, we need to grill it. I recommend wrapping the fish in foil and cooking it on the barbecue.

Serves 2

4 sardines, whole, but gutted and with scales removed

2 cloves of garlic, peeled and chopped

1 onion, peeled and sliced into rings

1 tbsp. dill, finely chopped

2 tbsp. olive oil

Juice of half a lemon
Salt and black pepper

Tear two pieces of foil, about 1 ft/30 cm square. Lay the foil squares flat on the work surface and place two fish into the centre of each. Divide the onion rings and garlic into two and pile onto the fish. Pour the olive oil and lemon juice over each pile and add generous pinches of salt and black pepper. Finally, top each pile with the dill.

Create secure parcels by bringing the two "long" edges of each foil piece together (that is, parallel with the fish) and fold to secure. Then fold over the ends of the parcels to seal.

Place both parcels on a smoking-hot barbecue. Cook for 10–15 minutes. Remove from the heat and unwrap on the plate. Serve with bread and a green salad.

Sea Bass with Seaweed and Rice

Sea bass with seaweed and rice, inspired by
You Only Live Twice (1964). Photo: Clare McIntyre

Rice with fish and seaweed is a typical lunch of the Ama fisher folk, with whom James Bond resides before leaving to enter Dr Shatterhand's "Garden of Death", described in the novel of *You Only Live Twice* (1964).[33] Bond well deserves his lunch; his catch of five awabi shells in a single session is an honourable one—for a gaijin. My version of this dish is something like a risotto. I've chosen sea bass, but this can be substituted by salmon, cod, haddock, sea bream or tuna. As for the seaweed, I suggest ready-prepared sheets of nori, which are typically used for sushi, but can be shredded.

Serves 2

5 oz./150 g. short grain rice
1 tbsp. vegetable oil
2 sea bass fillets, skin removed
3 cups/700 ml. fish stock
1 onion
1 tbsp. mirin
1 tbsp. soy sauce
1 tsp. brown sugar
2 sheets nori seaweed
Black pepper

Do a little preparation before cooking. Peel the onion and chop in half, then quarter each half so that you end up with chunky pieces. Finely chop the nori sheets. Create a sauce by combining the mirin, soy sauce, sugar, and a good pinch of black pepper in a small bowl. Make up the stock using a stock cube or prepare it fresh by boiling the skin, bones and head of the fish, if available, for 20 minutes, adding herbs and salt and pepper to flavour.

Heat the oil in a large saucepan or wok and gently fry the onion until it begins to take on some colour. Pour in the sauce, then add the rice and stir to coat the grains. Pour in the stock and bring to the boil. Reduce to a simmer, turning the rice around occasionally to prevent sticking.

After 10 minutes, cut the fish into bite-sized pieces and add to the wok, along with the shredded nori. Continue simmering, and occasionally stirring, for another 10 minutes until the rice has absorbed the stock and the nori has melted into the rice.

Shrimp Cocktail

With its garish pink and green hues and aroma of a lemon-scented wet-wipe, the shrimp (or prawn) cocktail dish is not quite the sophisticated dinner-party opener it once was. Even in 1965, when it's served at Scaramanga's Thunderbird Hotel in Jamaica in *The Man with the Golden Gun*, James Bond regards the shrimp cocktail as a merely conventional item of the Americanised hotel abroad.[34]

I think the shrimp cocktail has been out in the cold for long enough. It's time to restore the dish to classic status. The secret of a good shrimp cocktail is a crisp lettuce base and a sauce that complements the shellfish, not overwhelms it. For the former, I've gone with the dependable iceberg, and for the latter, a concoction based on a 1957 American recipe,[35] which brings a Bond-era taste to the dinner-party.

Serves 2–4

7 oz./200 g. cooked and peeled shrimps (chilled)
1 tsp. onion juice
1 tbsp. mayonnaise
1 tsp. chilli sauce
1 tsp. tomato purée
½ tsp. lemon juice
1 tbsp. red pepper, minced or very finely chopped
Salt and black pepper
Iceberg lettuce, shredded

To prepare the dressing, put the onion juice (peel and chop an onion, take a handful of the onion and squeeze), mayonnaise, chilli sauce, tomato purée, lemon juice, red pepper, and a pinch of salt and black pepper into a large bowl and combine well. Add the shrimps and stir until the shrimps are well coated with the dressing.

Assemble the dish by arranging some shredded lettuce on a small plate or the base of serving glasses. Spoon the shrimps on top. Chill for 30 minutes or so, then serve.

Shrimp Curry

Shrimp curry, as eaten by James Bond in
Goldfinger (1959). Photo: Clare McIntyre

Goldfinger assures Bond that the curry that Oddjob serves is shrimp, not cat. You can't blame Bond for checking; Oddjob's rather fond of cats, and Bond's just seen him enter the kitchen with a ginger tom under his arm.[36] Bond enjoys the curry as a starter, but the dish deserves to be upgraded to a main meal. I've gone back to basics with this recipe. Chilli peppers, native to the Americas, are out and replaced by Asian peppercorns. It's a straight swap; the peppercorns provide all the heat you'll need.

Serves 2

For the curry paste:
1 onion
Peppercorns (3 tsp. for hot, 2 tsp. for medium, 1 tsp. for mild)
1 tsp. fennel seeds
1 tsp. cardamom pods
1 tsp. cumin seeds
1 tsp. coriander seeds
½ tsp. turmeric powder
⅓ tsp. fenugreek powder
½ tsp. cinnamon powder
1 tsp. white wine vinegar
For the curry:
1 tbsp. ghee
5 oz./150 g. natural yoghurt
⅝ cup/150 ml. fish stock
7 oz./200 g. peeled shrimps (frozen is fine)
1 tbsp. fresh coriander
Salt

Grind the whole spices in a mortar or electric grinder and tip into a bowl (removing, if necessary, the cardamom pod shells). Add the powdered spices and the vinegar. Roughly chop the onion and purée in a food processor. Mix the onion with the spices to create a paste.

Heat and melt the ghee on a medium heat in a saucepan or karahi. Gently add the spice paste and fry for 2 to 3 minutes. Take the pan off the heat and fold in the yoghurt gradually; add a tablespoon or two, stir it in and allow it to reduce and become absorbed into the spices before adding more yoghurt.

Drop in the shrimps, stirring them around the pan to coat them with the sauce. Pour in the stock, stir, then bring to a furious simmer. Cook the curry for about 10 minutes, stirring occasionally, until the sauce has thickened and reduced by half. Just before the curry's ready, add salt to taste, then finely chop the fresh coriander and drop into the pan, partially folding the herbs into the sauce.

Smoked Salmon

We know that, in the novels, James Bond loves smoked salmon and regards Scottish smoked salmon as the finest. In *Moonraker* (1955), for example, he tells M, while dining at M's club, Blades, that he has a mania for the dish. The salmon that's served is described as having a glutinous texture only achieved by Scottish curers. Scandinavian products are, in contrast, dismissed as being desiccated. In *Diamonds are Forever* (1956), Bond is served smoked salmon from Nova Scotia at Sardi's in New York. The salmon is described as a poor substitute for the product of Scotland.[37]

It comes as little surprise that Bond shared his taste of smoked salmon with his creator; in his "Atticus" column published in the *Sunday Times* on 31st July 1955, Ian Fleming wrote that there was no doubt that smoked salmon cured in Scotland was the finest in the world.[38]

Next time you have smoked salmon, serve the slices with buttered brown bread, just as Bond has it in Blades (silver tray optional).

Snapper

Red snapper, possibly the way James Bond might have cooked it in *No Time to Die* (2021). Photo: Author

James Bond (Daniel Craig) takes up fishing with a speargun during his retiring in Jamaica in *No Time to Die* (2021). In the film, we see the fruits of his labours, as, having returned from a fishing trip, he carries a couple of what appear to be red snapper back to his home in a lagoon. The choice of fish is an appropriate one: snapper was regularly on the menu at Ian Fleming's Jamaican home, *Goldeneye*.[39] Unfortunately, we never find out how James Bond cooks the fish, but it might have been on the lines of this recipe inspired by one that appeared in the pages of James Bond's favourite newspaper, Jamaica's *Daily Gleaner*.[40]

Serves 2

2 red snapper loin steaks (or fillets)
Juice and zest of 1 orange
1–2 cloves of garlic, peeled and chopped
1 tbsp. olive oil

Generous pinch each of black pepper and salt
Pinch finely chopped parsley

Combine the orange juice, oil, salt, pepper and garlic in a large bowl. Lay the steaks in the bowl and ensure that they are well covered by the liquid. Marinate the fish ideally for several hours.

Heat the oven to 375°F (190°C; 170°C fan-assisted). Lightly oil the base of an oven dish. Place the steaks in the dish skin-side up, shaking off the excess marinade. Put the dish in the oven and cook for 15–20 minutes.

About five minutes before the end of the cooking time, pour the marinade into a small saucepan and, over a medium heat, reduce the liquid by half. Strain the marinade—now sauce—into a small bowl.

To serve, spoon the sauce neatly onto a couple of plates. Lay the red snapper steaks onto the sauce, and sprinkle the parsley and orange zest over the top.

Soft-Shell Crabs with Tartare Sauce

James Bond enjoys a plate of soft-shell crabs, served with tartare sauce, in the novel of *Live and Let Die* (1954), not long after arriving in New York and checking into the St. Regis Hotel.[41] In *A View to a Kill* (1985), James Bond (Roger Moore) asks for soft-shell crabs at Fisherman's Wharf in San Francisco, although in this case he's after information, not a meal; the request is a recognition phrase to establish contact with a CIA operative, Chuck Lee (David Yip).

Soft-shell crabs are typically blue crabs caught immediately after moulting. In the US, the blue crab season runs from April to September, which, if the crabs are fresh, tells us something about when Bond adventures are taking place. Frozen crabs are of course available all-year round. Once cleaned (the gills removed, the "apron" cut out etc), the entire crab is edible, shell, legs and all. Soft-shell crabs are best cooked simply. In my recipe, I dust the crabs in flour and shallow fry them. Tartare sauce is usually made from mayonnaise, but here, as an alternative, I use a hollandaise base. The sauce can be prepared in advance.

Serves 2

    4 soft-shell crabs, cleaned
    Seasoned plain flour
    Oil for frying
    For the sauce:
    2 egg yolks
    1 tbsp. lemon juice
    1 tbsp. water
    4 oz./100 g. unsalted butter, cut into chunks
    1 tsp. finely chopped parsley
    1 tsp. finely chopped capers
    1 tsp. finely chopped gherkins

First, prepare the sauce. Bring a saucepan of water to the boil. Turn the heat to the lowest setting or switch off altogether so that there are no bubbles, only steam, emanating from the water. Put the yolks, lemon juice and the tablespoon of water into a bowl and place the bowl on top of the saucepan. Whisk the ingredients until the sauce become smooth and creamy. Add the butter a piece at a time, whisking each piece until it has been fully absorbed into the sauce before adding the next piece. Continue whisking for about 10 minutes until all the butter has been absorbed and the sauce has thickened. Remove the bowl from the saucepan and allow the sauce to cool in the refrigerator. Once the sauce has cooled, stir in the parsley, capers and gherkins and return the sauce to the refrigerator.

    Pat the crabs dry. Heat some cooking oil in a frying pan, using enough oil to cover the base. Roll the crabs in the seasoned flour, then place each crab in the pan, top side down. Fry the crabs for 3–4 minutes, then turn them over and continue frying for another 3–4 minutes. Transfer the crabs to plates and spoon a generous helping of tartare sauce on the side.

Sole (Fried)

In the novel of *Moonraker* (1955), having narrowly escaped death when a portion of the white cliffs near Dover almost fell on top of them as they lay on the beach, James Bond and Special Branch agent Gala Brand head to the Granville hotel in St Margaret's Bay for several restorative brandies-and-soda, followed by delicious fried soles and Welsh rarebit.[42] The fish is typically Dover sole, but other types, such as lemon sole, make acceptable (and cheaper) alternatives.

Moonraker, Ian Fleming's third Bond novel, has the distinction of being the first adventure that mentions sole, a fish to which Bond is very partial; he admits in *On Her Majesty's Secret Service* (1963) that he practically lives on grilled sole while at home in London between missions.[43] It's a fondness that survives into the film series: James Bond (Sean Connery) orders grilled sole in the restaurant car of the *Orient Express* in *From Russia with Love* (1963).

Serves 2

2 fillets, skin removed, from 1 Dover sole
2 tbsp. seasoned flour
Vegetable and butter for frying
Lemon wedges
Sprigs of parsley

Place a frying pan over a high heat. Coat the base of a frying pan with the oil and add a knob of butter. As the oil and butter are heating up, dust both sides of a fillet with the flour; give the fish a gentle shake to remove excess flour. Lay the fillet in the pan (I'm assuming your pan won't be large enough for both fillets) and fry for 3–4 minutes on each side. Transfer the fish to a plate and keep it warm. Top up the oil and butter and dust and fry the second fillet. When serving, garnish the fish with a couple of wedges of lemon and a sprig or two of parsley.

Sole Meunière

In the novel of *Goldfinger* (1959), we learn that, when travelling through France, James Bond likes to dine at railway station restaurants, where there was a good chance that the food would be excellent. Naturally, then, when stopping overnight in Orléans during his epic drive through France and into Switzerland in pursuit of Goldfinger, Bond dines at the *Buffet de la Gare*, enjoying two oeufs cocotte à la crème, a sole meunière (literally sole cooked in the "miller's wife style"), and an "adequate" Camembert.[44]

James Bond's view of station buffets did not simply reflect Ian Fleming's own preferences. Thanks to an initiative of the French National Railway Company (SNCF), station restaurants had long enjoyed a reputation for serving good, regional dishes at reasonable prices. Such restaurants were identified as "buffets gastronomiques" and they included the buffet at Orléans station. Typically, a meal at a buffet would comprise soup or an hors d'oeuvre, a fish or egg dish, a meat dish, some cheese, and, to finish, a piece of fruit or some ice cream—all for between an economical 600 and 765 francs.[45]

So much for the idea that James Bond dines only at the most exclusive establishments. Bond's meal largely follows this menu, consisting of, as it does, an egg dish, a meat dish (in the form of fish), and some cheese. Alas, the *Buffet de la Gare* no longer exists, but it is still possible to find the dish among the many restaurants in the city.

Serves 2

2 fillets, skin removed, from 1 Dover sole
For the sauce:
2 oz./50 g. butter
Juice from ½ lemon
1 tbsp. fresh parsley

Fry the soles as above. Alternatively, brush one side of both fillets with melted butter and place the fish under a hot grill (buttered side towards the heat) for 3–4 minutes. Turn the fish over, brush with butter and grill for the same time again.

To prepare the sauce, melt the butter in a saucepan over a high heat. Allow the butter to sizzle and bubble. When the butter begins to turn brown, add the lemon juice and parsley. Swirl the sauce around to allow the ingredients to mix, and then take the pan off the heat.

Transfer the fillets to plates and spoon the sauce generously over the fish.

Stone Crabs

James Bond may consume scrambled eggs with the frequency of someone who can't get enough of the dish, declare grilled lamb cutlets to be excellent, or enjoy the best cut of the finest meat in America, but the most delicious meal he has ever had in his life is none of these. That honour goes to a heap of stone crabs, accompanied by melted butter, dry toast, and Champagne, which Bond has at Bill's on the Beach restaurant in Miami in *Goldfinger* (1959).[46]

Florida stone crabs are famed for the large size of their claws, which are typically served on their own. If stone crabs are unobtainable, the legs and claws of king crabs or snow crabs make an excellent alternative (as James Bond and his dinner companion, Mr. Du Pont, may themselves have concluded during their discussion in the novel of the comparative merits of stone crabs and Alaskan king crabs).

For the recipe here, I've opted for king crabs. A single king crab leg is a good portion for one person, although for an indulgent meal worthy of James Bond, I'd recommend two or three legs per person.

Be warned: this is a messy dish. Normally I'd hesitate to wear a bib, even one made of silk, but if a bib's good enough for James Bond, it's good enough for us mere mortals.

King crabs, a good alternative to stone crabs, as featured in *Goldfinger* (1959). Photo: Author

Serves 2–3

    1 lb./1 kg. raw king crab sections
    4 oz./120 g (or more if wished) butter
    1 clove garlic, finely chopped
    1 tsp. lemon juice

Pinch finely chopped parsley
4 slices bread
Olive oil

Heat the grill or the make the barbecue ready for cooking. Brush the crab sections with a little olive oil, then place under or on the heat. Cook for about 15 minutes, turning over the crab sections halfway through the cooking time. Once cooked, transfer the crab to a serving dish.

Melt the butter in a saucepan over a high heat, adding the garlic, lemon juice and parsley. While the butter's melting, toast the bread. When the butter is bubbling away, remove it from the heat and pour it into a jug or individual bowls. If there's room, place the jug and dry toast onto the dish with the crab and serve. To enjoy the crab, use nutcrackers or scissors to open up the shell.

Stone crab claws can be cooked in the same way, except that the cooking time should be reduced to 10 minutes.

Tuna Baguette

Food has provided a few laughs in the James Bond films. We can think of, for example, the bombe surprise in *Diamonds Are Forever* (1971), where the bombe is actually a bomb. Or there's Q's lunch in *GoldenEye* (1995). At the end of a briefing by Q (Desmond Llewelyn) in his lab, James Bond (Pierce Brosnan) spots a filled baguette, picks it up and examines it, wondering what mystery gadget it conceals. Q snatches the baguette off him. "Don't touch that!" Q exclaims, as if Bond had been casually handling a deadly device. "That's my lunch."

In the novelisation of the film by John Gardner, the baguette is described as six or seven inches of a French stick, cut in two and filled with tuna, tomatoes and onions.[47] If this had been taken from the script, the catering company or prop team responsible for the sandwich can't have read it very closely, because Q's baguette seems much longer than six or seven inches. It also contains cucumber and lettuce, as well as tomatoes, but doesn't appear to have any onions. It's hard to see whether the baguette contains tuna, but as there's no ham or other sliced meat protruding from the edges of the baguette, it's entirely possible that it does.

Whatever its precise contents, a Q-style baguette is easy to make. Cut a generous length from a baguette or take a half baguette. Slice it in half lengthwise from the side, butter the halves and spread tuna (mixed with mayonnaise if wished) onto the bottom half. Pile some shredded iceberg lettuce, sliced tomatoes and sliced cucumber on top, season with a bit of black pepper, and replace the upper half of the baguette.

4. Meat and Poultry

Angels on Horseback

James Bond confirms that his taste buds are aligned towards the savoury end of the spectrum with a non-sweet dish to follow a main course during his dinner chez Dr. No in the novel of *Dr. No* (1958).[1] Angels on horseback are bite-sized parcels of bacon and oysters, and make an excellent canapé, if you're not so fussed about having them to finish a meal.

Serves 2

> 8 smoked oysters (tinned)
> 4 rashers unsmoked bacon
> Black pepper
> Lemon juice
> Butter for frying

Trim the fat from the bacon and cut each rasher into two strips. Take a strip, lay an oyster onto it, sprinkle with a little pepper, and roll the bacon around the oyster. Repeat for the other seven. Fry the parcels gently in butter, turning occasionally, for 2 to 3 minutes until the bacon is cooked. Garnish with some chopped parsley and serve with toast or fried bread.

Brizzola

James Bond is treated to brizzola for lunch at Sardi's in New York during the events of the novel of *Diamonds Are Forever* (1956).[2] Brizzola in essence is a cut of beef that has been roasted then charcoal-grilled. Typically, steaks are sliced from a roasted prime rib of beef, but for economy (the recipe serves two) and for sheer melt-in-the-mouth flavour, I am using beef short ribs. This dish is inspired by a recipe by one Mr. William Joy that appeared in *Grosse Pointe News* in October 1947.[3] If using steaks, then cook a rib of beef according to standard guidelines, cut it into slices, then follow the recipe below from the second paragraph.

Serves 2

 2 beef short ribs
 ⅝ cup/150 ml. water or beef stock
 For the marinade:
 2–3 tbsp. vegetable oil
 2 generous pinches of salt
 2 generous pinches of black pepper
 For the sauce:
 2 oz./50 g. butter
 1 tsp. parsley, finely chopped
 1 tsp. chives, finely chopped

Heat the oven to 330°F (170°C; 150°C fan-assisted). Pour the stock or water into a lidded oven dish or roasting tin. Place the beef ribs in the dish and cover the dish with a lid or foil. Put the dish in the oven and cook for 2½ hours.

Transfer the ribs to a bowl and add the oil, salt and pepper. Turn the ribs over so that they are well coated. Leave the ribs until they cool down, then put the bowl in the refrigerator for 3–5 hours or overnight.

Prepare the grill or barbecue for cooking. Remove the ribs from the bowl and place them above or below the hot grill as required. Cook the ribs for 5–8 minutes, turning them occasionally to ensure that all the surfaces are exposed to or are in contact with the grill. When the ribs are sizzling, transfer them to serving plates.

While the ribs are grilling, prepare a brown butter sauce. Melt the butter in a saucepan above a high heat. Let the butter bubble for a few minutes until it begins to turn brown. Add the parsley and chives. Pour the sauce over the ribs and serve.

Butter-Basted Chicken with Watercress

After arriving at the Royal Bahamian hotel in Nassau during the events of the novel of *Thunderball* (1961), James Bond and Felix Leiter consult the hotel menu and order lunch. Bond opts for "home farm" broiled chicken, disjointed and basted with creamery butter, and "sauté au cresson" (priced 38/6 or $5.35).[4] The dish appears to be based on the French classic, poulet rôti au beurre, a standard in contemporary cookbooks such as Elizabeth David's *French Provincial Cooking* (1960) or Mary Reynolds' *French Cooking for Pleasure* (1966).[5] Bond and Leiter are disappointed with their lunches, but you can't go far wrong with this recipe.

Serves 4

1 chicken, oven-ready with giblets removed
2½ oz./60 g. butter
A handful of herbs, such as a bay leaf and sprigs of rosemary, parsley, thyme or marjoram
Salt and pepper
4 oz./100 g. watercress, coarsely chopped

Heat the oven to 375°F (190°C; 170°C fan-assisted). Stuff the cavity with the herbs, half the butter and a good pinch of salt and pepper. Rest the chicken on its side in a roasting tin and rub the skin with the rest of the butter, putting any remaining bits of butter underneath the chicken. Place the chicken in the oven. After 20 minutes, turn the chicken over onto its other side and baste the exposed side with the juices and melted butter. Cook the chicken for another 20 minutes before placing it breast-side up and basting again. Continue cooking for another 20 to 30 minutes until the chicken is cooked (the juices should be running clear).

Remove the chicken from the roasting tin. Cut the chicken into six to eight pieces (two legs, two thighs and up to two portions per breast) and place the pieces onto a serving dish. Put the dish to one side. Place the roasting tin on the hob (or pour the juices from the tin into a saucepan) and heat the juices until they begin to bubble. Add the watercress and sauté until it wilts (it should be a matter of seconds). Drizzle the resulting watercress sauce over the chicken and serve.

Cassoulet

Though James Bond is clearly a lover of French food, there are lacunae in his gastronomic experiences. One such gap is cassoulet, the famous pork, bean and duck (or goose) stew of southwest France, which is never mentioned in Ian Fleming's novels. The closest Bond has come to it is a tin of Heinz pork and beans in the novel of *Dr. No* (1958). However, in Christopher Wood's novelisation of the film of *The Spy Who Loved Me* (1977), Bond discovers tins of cassoulet in a cupboard in a mountain hut in Chamonix.

Unfortunately, he doesn't have a chance to sample any of them, as he is ambushed by some men who want to kill him.[6]

As is usually the case for traditional dishes, there are many variations of cassoulet, and the version below is something of an amalgam of several of them. I've used garlic sausage, which tends to be specified in older recipes, but these days Toulouse sausage is more typical. The older recipes also call for lamb or mutton, but I have to say that on none of the very many occasions I've had cassoulet, including in the old town of Carcassonne, where the dish is a speciality and restaurants offering the dish line the old streets, has it ever included mutton. I've cut the sausage and pork belly into bite-size pieces, as befitting the tins that Bond encounters.

Serves 5–6

14 oz./400 g. pork belly, excess fat trimmed and cut into small pieces

7 oz./200 g. garlic sausage, cut into small pieces

14 oz./400 g. duck confit

2 tins (1.7 lb./800 g. undrained weight) cannellini beans, drained

1 medium onion, peeled and chopped

1 bay leaf

1 tbsp. herbes de Provence or 1 tsp. each of, say, marjoram, thyme, rosemary and parsley

Pinch of black pepper

1 cup/200 ml. vegetable or chicken stock

Heat the oven to 375°F (190°C; 170°C fan-assisted). Fry the onion in a little vegetable oil until it has softened. (If cooking dry beans, the onion should be cooked with them.)

In a large oven pot, casserole or, better still, a cassole, the traditional cassoulet vessel, place the onion, herbs, pepper, meat and beans. Stir gently to mix the ingredients together and pour in the stock until the liquid is about half-way up the pot.

Cover the pot with a lid and transfer the pot to the oven. Cook for about 1½ hours. After about 1 hour, remove the lid (I sometimes spoon out 1 or 2 ladles of the stock at this point if it looks like there is a bit too much liquid) to allow a crust to form on the top.

At the end of the cooking time, remove the pot from the oven and serve with a crusty baguette.

Choucroute Garnie

Geneva as described in *Goldfinger* (1959): the Pont
du Mont Blanc and, located to the left of the far end
of the bridge, the Hotel des Bergues. Photo: Author

Deciding on dinner, following his marathon drive through France
and into Switzerland in pursuit of Goldfinger in the novel of *Goldfinger* (1959), James Bond eschews the opulent surroundings of Geneva's
Hotel des Bergues, where he is staying, and opts instead for the rustic
and hearty offerings of the nearby Bavaria, a comfortable brasserie
situated at 49 rue du Rhône.[7] Ian Fleming tells us that Bond has choucroute,[8] but assuming Bond doesn't simply chomp his way through
a plate of pickled cabbage, it's more reasonable to imagine that he
has choucroute garnie—sauerkraut liberally garnished with assorted
pork products and a speciality of the Alsace region of France.

Serves 3–4

1½ lbs/650 g. sauerkraut (approx. 1 lb./450 g. drained)
1 medium carrot, peeled and sliced
1 onion, peeled and sliced into rings

Generous pinch of black pepper

4 oz./100 g. smoked lardons

2–4 juniper berries, crushed

1½ oz./30 g. butter

⅝ cup/150 ml. white wine (preferably Alsace)

2½ cups/600 ml. vegetable stock or water

5 oz./150 g. garlic sausage, sliced

3 or 4 slices of pork belly

1 lb./450 g. potatoes

4–6 frankfurters

Heat the oven to 300°F (170°C; 150°C fan-assisted). On the hob, melt the butter in a casserole or deep oven-proof dish. Over a medium flame, fry the onion, carrot, and lardons until the onion has softened. Meanwhile, drain the sauerkraut, rinse thoroughly and squeeze out excess liquid. Add the sauerkraut to the casserole, along with the black pepper and juniper berries. Mix the ingredients well and pour in the stock or water and wine. Cover the casserole with a lid and place it in the oven.

After 2 hours, remove the casserole from the oven, remove the lid and bury the pork belly slices within the mixture and stir in the garlic sausage. Cover the casserole again and put it back into the oven for another 2 hours.

With 1 hour remaining, peel the potatoes, cut them in half or quarters, depending on size, and boil them in salted water until cooked. Drain the potatoes and put them aside.

With about 15–20 minutes cooking time left, remove the casserole from the oven, lift the lid and gently fold the potatoes and frankfurters into the sauerkraut. Cover and return the dish to the oven for the remaining time.

Remove the casserole from the oven and serve. Accompany servings with Löwenbrau or the remaining Alsace wine. If at any stage of the cooking, the sauerkraut seems too dry, add a little more liquid.

Doner Kebab

While Kerim Bey tucks into steak tartare in Istanbul's Spice Bazaar, James Bond enjoys a doner kebab, which Kerim describes as young lamb broiled over charcoal and served with rice and lots of onions.[9] Today the standard fare of the nocturnal post-pub crowd and traditionally deposited half-consumed on the pavement, the doner kebab was, when *From Russia with Love* (1957) was published, considered a rather more exotic and sophisticated dish. It is difficult to replicate a doner kebab at home without a vertical rotisserie or gyro, but my recipe should produce a reasonable facsimile of an unfairly devalued dish.

Serves 2

1 lb./500 g. minced lamb
1 tsp. chopped thyme
1 tsp. smoked paprika
2 cloves garlic, peeled and chopped
1 tsp. olive oil
Pinch of salt
Pinch of black pepper
1 onion, peeled and sliced into rings
Vegetable oil for frying

In a mortar, grind the garlic and salt into a paste. Put the mince, garlic paste, paprika, thyme, olive oil and a generous pinch of black pepper into a mixing bowl. With your hands, combine all the ingredients and shape the mixture into a fat sausage. Refrigerate the mince for a few hours.

Push a skewer through the centre of the mince lengthwise and place the kebab under or on the grill, or on a barbecue. Cook the kebab for about 30 minutes, turning regularly. Meanwhile, gently fry the onions in the vegetable oil.

To serve, shave slivers of meat from the sides of the kebab or slice the kebab thinly. Pile the onions on top.

Fried Chicken Maryland

Always willing to sample the essential flavours of the places he visits, James Bond happily consumes a plate of fried chicken Maryland at New York's Ma Frazier's in *Live and Let Die* (1954). Well, it is the national dish, according to his American contact and local guide Felix Leiter.[10]

For many years, I pictured James Bond picking up pieces of breadcrumbed chicken, Kentucky Fried Chicken-style. In fact, according to cookbooks contemporary with, or earlier than, Bond's American adventure, the chicken pieces in the dish weren't originally coated in breadcrumbs but flour only and were accompanied by a cream sauce. Naturally, then, I've looked to those older cookbooks for inspiration for my recipe. The recipe below has been adapted from one submitted by a Miss E. J. Thomas to a volume of American recipes published in 1901.[11]

Incidentally, there is a connection between Kentucky Fried Chicken and James Bond. One of Colonel Sanders' restaurants appears in the background of a scene in the film of *Goldfinger* (1964), having been spotted by director Guy Hamilton and featured to give local colour to the film.[12] The restaurant would have been unremarkable to cinemagoers in the USA, where outlets of the chain were widespread, but for UK audiences, it was a sign of things to come: Kentucky Fried Chicken opened its first restaurant in Great Britain the following year in 1965.[13]

Serves 3–4

1 chicken, cut into eight pieces (two legs, two thighs and two portions per breast)

Plain flour, seasoned

1 cup/250 ml. double cream
1 tbsp. parsley, coarsely chopped
1 tbsp. marjoram, finely chopped
Salt and black pepper
Vegetable oil for frying

Heat the oil in a deep, frying pan or wide saucepan, using enough oil to generously cover the base of the pan. Coat the chicken pieces in flour, shaking off any excess. Lay the pieces in the pan (skin-side down initially) and fry over a fairly gentle heat for approximately 25 minutes, turning occasionally, until cooked and golden brown. (If the juices run pink when the meat is pricked, continue cooking until the juices are clear.)

Take the pan off the heat. Transfer the chicken pieces to a serving dish with absorbent paper on the base and keep warm. Remove all but a tablespoon of the juices in the pan. Pour in the cream, stir, then return the pan to the heat. Add the parsley and marjoram and a good pinch of salt and pepper. Heat the sauce through, then pour into a jug.

Serve the chicken with bacon and sweetcorn and a generous helping of the sauce.

Grilled Kidney

The breakfast that James Bond consumes in the novel of *Dr. No* (1958), having been captured on Crab Key by the eponymous villain and welcomed into a "mink-lined prison", is the closest Bond gets in the books to a "full English". Presented on an individual hotplate are scrambled eggs on toast, four rashers of bacon, a grilled kidney, and an English pork sausage. These are accompanied by two kinds of toast, rolls, strawberry jam, marmalade, honey, pineapple juice and coffee with cream.[14] After consuming this feast, Bond begins to feel sleepy. He blames the coffee or juice, one of which he suspects has been drugged, but a substantial breakfast like that would make anyone want to crawl back into bed.

Per person

1 lamb's kidney, cleaned
A large knob of unsalted butter
Black pepper
Salt

Heat the grill. While the grill is heating up, melt the butter in a saucepan. Cut the kidney in half lengthwise and carefully remove the whitish core. Lay the kidney halves on a grill pan cut-side up and brush the surface with the butter, then sprinkle some salt and pepper over them. Put the kidney under the grill and cook for 3–4 minutes. Turn the kidney halves over and brush more butter on top and season. Grill for another 3–4 minutes. The kidney can be eaten slightly pink in the middle. Serve with bacon, a sausage and scrambled eggs.

Hamburger

The St. Regis Hotel, New York, visited by James Bond in
Live and Let Die (1954). Photo: Author

Today, the hamburger is readily dismissed as junk food, a highly processed, homogenized, and globalized meat patty. In the 1950s, however, the hamburger was still sufficiently exotic and regional, at least for visitors to the USA, for Ian Fleming to include it in James Bond's quintessentially American meal, along with soft-shell crabs and ice-cream with butterscotch sauce, at New York's St. Regis Hotel in *Live and Let Die* (1954). In the text, Bond consumes what are described as "flat beef Hamburgers."[15] He clearly has more than one, but how many (two? three?) is uncertain. And are Bond's burgers encased in buns? Again, we don't know, although I suspect that the burgers are presented without the usual trimmings.

Hamburgers are on the menu in the Fillet of Soul bar and restaurant in the film of *Live and Let Die* (1973). When James Bond (Roger Moore) enters, he is directed to a booth, behind which is a menu painted on the wall. If he hadn't had a nasty turn in the booth, Bond could have bought a hamburger for 65–75 cents, or a cheeseburger for 70–80 cents. The scene shows Bond as a fish out of water; as Bond enters, the people at the bar stop their conversations and all eyes follow him to the bar. The menu serves to reinforce Bond's discomfort, and briefly Bond appears to study the menu as if unfamiliar with the options. With no caviar, grilled sole or café complet on offer, this is a different world to the one he's used to.

The recipe here is adapted from one published in 1957, just a few years after the publication of *Live and Let Die*.[16] It's possible that Bond's burger or, rather, the burgers that Fleming is likely to have eaten during his visits to the country, tasted something like this.

Makes 3–4 burgers

  1 lb./450 g. beef steak mince
  1 tbsp. grated onion
  1 tbsp. tomato ketchup
  1 tsp. mustard

½ tsp. horseradish sauce
A pinch each of salt and black pepper

Put all the ingredients in a bowl and mix until they are well combined. Divide the mixture into three or four portions, depending on how large you like your burgers; the mixture comfortably makes three thick burgers. Mould each one by hand into a burger shape or press into a chef's ring to create a neat disc. (On removing the chef's ring, gently press the burger to make it thinner and wider if necessary.) Refrigerate the burgers for about 20 minutes.

Place the burgers under a hot grill or, better still, on a charcoal grill or barbecue and cook for 4 minutes on each side (for medium rare), or a little longer if preferred. Allow the burgers to rest for a few minutes before serving.

Lamb Cutlets

When James Bond eats lamb cutlets at M's club, Blades, in *Moonraker* (1955), he declares, having judged the cutlets to be superb, that the best English cooking is the best in the world. A bold claim, given that he thought the cutlets he was served while in Dr. No's clutches in the novel of the same name (1958) to be excellent. At Dr. No's place, the cutlets are accompanied by a salad, but at Blades, they come with peas, new potatoes and asparagus.[17] Ian Fleming was rather partial to the dish himself; he served lamb cutlets and asparagus to the real James Bond—the American ornithologist whose name Fleming appropriated for his here—at Goldeneye in 1964.[18]

Serves 2

4 lamb cutlets
Olive oil
Salt and black pepper

Brush the cutlets with olive oil, season, then grill for 6–7 minutes each side. It's as simple as that.

Lyon Sausage

St. Laurent-sur-Saône, France, where James Bond has a run-in
with Tilly Masterton in *Goldfinger* (1959). Photo: Author

James Bond's epic car journey from Le Touquet to Geneva in pursuit of Goldfinger in Ian Fleming's 1959 novel is not only one of the great literary journeys, but also a veritable gastronomic tour, where even minor stops along the way offer a taste of the region.

When James Bond approaches the centre of Mâcon, some 100 miles west of Geneva, he spots Goldfinger's Rolls Royce ahead of him on Rue Rambuteau and follows Goldfinger over a railway bridge, through a little square (Place de la Barre) and across the bridge over the River Saône into the suburb of St Laurent-sur-Saône. Once there, Bond decides to take the Triumph driven by Tilly Masterton, who's also after Goldfinger, out of the equation by reversing his Aston Martin into it. The collision gives Bond the opportunity to pick up some items for lunch and he asks Masterton to buy six inches of Lyon sausage from a butcher's shop with the golden calf's head sign, a loaf of bread and half a litre of Mâcon wine for him and whatever Masterton wants for herself.[19]

The butcher's shop has long since gone, but it's still possible to buy the items from the local stores, among them a tabac on the main road and small supermarket in a side street. Once purchased, return to your car, and continue southeast on the N79 (formerly the D1079) towards Geneva via Bourg-en-Bresse on Goldfinger's trail.

Marrow Bone

As revealed in *Moonraker* (1955), M's rather
partial to marrow bone. Photo: Author

While ordering dinner at his club, Blades, in the novel of *Moonraker* (1955), M is persuaded by the head steward to have a marrow bone after his dessert of strawberries. He confesses to the steward that he can't resist them.[20] Marrow bones can be cut across the bone to form a tube and presented on their ends (as in M's case) or chopped in half along the length of the bone. M's marrow bone, propped up with a lace napkin, appears to be without accompaniments, but for a slightly more substantial dish, serve the bone with toast and some capers, or, as I suggest below, caperberries.

Serves 2

> 2 beef marrow bones
> Finely chopped parsley
> Salt and pepper
> 2 slices toast
> 6–8 caperberries

Heat the oven to 430°F (220°C; 200°C fan-assisted). Lay the marrow bones in an oven dish or deep baking tray. Sprinkle parsley, salt and pepper over the tops of the bones and place the dish or tray in the oven. Cook for 20 minutes, by which time the marrow should be bubbling and slightly puffy. Transfer the bones to plates and serve with toast and caperberries.

Melon with Prosciutto Ham

While James Bond is eating tagliatelle verdi during the events of "Risico" (1960), Kristatos has melon accompanied by prosciutto, an Italian dry-cured ham.[21] This light dish makes an excellent starter, and what is more, the melon and ham need little preparation.

Serves 2

> 2 slices melon, such as cantaloupe or charentais
> 6 slices prosciutto
> Black pepper
> Basil-infused olive oil

Take two slices from the melon and remove the seeds. Neatly cut the flesh of both slices into sections across the width, taking care not to cut into the skin. Carefully slide the knife along the inside of the skin to remove the melon pieces. Reassemble the pieces and put the slices onto plates. Crack some pepper over the slices. Roll or fold the prosciutto slices (I've suggested three per person) and place them onto the plates with the melon. Drizzle a little olive oil over the ham and serve.

Mutton Ragout

At a Gypsy camp on the outskirts of Istanbul in *From Russia with Love* (1957), James Bond is served "some sort of ragout", which he finds delicious. It's a simple rustic dish and a perfect entrée before the main event: a fight between two Gypsy women, rivals in love.[22] The girl-fight is optional, but the traditional Turkish stew, a combination of meat and a lot of small onions, is essential eating. The dish below is inspired by a Turkish recipe for a ragout, which was first published in 1958 and is almost exactly contemporary with Bond's meal.[23] That recipe calls for mutton, but lamb or beef will do just as well.

Serves 2–3

12 oz./350 g. diced mutton or lamb
2 tbsp. olive oil
Approx. 15 shallots or baby onions
2 cloves garlic, chopped
1¼ cups/300 ml. lamb stock
⅝ cup/150 ml. red wine
1 tbsp. parsley
½ tbsp. thyme
1 tsp. dill
Salt and pepper
Seasoned flour

Peel the onions, leaving them whole. Finely chop the garlic and herbs. Heat the oil in a heavy saucepan or flame-proof casserole and fry the onions on a low heat for 5 minutes until they take on a brown, caramelised appearance. Meanwhile, coat the mutton in the flour.

Add the meat and let it brown for a minute or two, then pour in the wine and stir. Raise the heat if necessary to bring the liquid to the boil, then add the stock, garlic, a pinch of salt and pepper, thyme and half the parsley. Return the liquid to the boil, then cover the pan, reduce the heat and simmer on a low heat for about 1½ hours, stirring occasionally.

Just before taking the stew off the heat, stir in the dill and the rest of the parsley. Serve with coarse, chunky bread.

Pâté de Foie Gras

A controversial dish here; pâté de foie gras divides people like no other food. Literally "fatted liver", the pâté is traditionally made of the livers of ducks or geese which have been force-fed to fatten them up ("gavage"). To many, the process is a grotesque distortion of acceptable farming methods; others counter that the animals at many farms are well looked after and typically enjoy a free-range, if not entirely stress-free, life, and that feeding can be carried out humanely to reduce animal discomfort as much as possible (battery methods become illegal in France in 2010).

In Ian Fleming's day, there were few concerns about animal welfare, and James Bond consumes foie gras with relish, beginning in *Casino Royale* (1953).[24] An "excellent" foie gras is one of the goodies in the Harrods hamper that James Bond (Timothy Dalton) assembles for General Georgi Koskov (Jeroen Krabbé) in the film of *The Living Daylights* (1987).

The recipe below was given to me, via my wife's French aunt, by an elderly resident of southwest France, the heart of foie gras country, and is of some antiquity.

Serves several

2 lb./1 kg. duck livers
1 oz./18 g. sea salt

1 tsp. ground pepper
1 tsp. black or green peppercorns
Truffle, to taste (gratings or essence)

Soak the livers for 2 hours in cold water and remove blood vessels. Dry the livers, then cover with the salt and leave for 12–15 hours, turning occasionally.

Wash the livers to remove salt, finely chop the liver and mix with the black pepper, peppercorns and truffle and place in a sterilising bottle, or more than one depending on size (sterilised jam jars can be used instead). Put the bottle in a saucepan of gently boiling water and boil for 20 minutes. Smaller bottles require less time, around 10–15 minutes.

Turn the heat off and allow to rest in the pan for 10 to 15 minutes. Remove the bottles and cool overnight. Turn the foie gras out of the bottles and press into a pâté dish or terrine. Refrigerate for at least two days. For connoisseurs, who prefer their foie gras "mi-cuit", reduce the cooking time by half.

Pâté Maison

We learn at the beginning of the novel of *On Her Majesty's Secret Service* (1963) that before reaching Royale-les-Eaux on his way back from a fruitless hunt for Blofeld, James Bond had stopped overnight at an auberge on the south bank of the Loire. There he received a kicking from the "French belly-religion", having been offered a sleazy provender of, among other dishes, an out-of-season poularde à la crème and the fly-walk of the pâté maison, which Bond was obliged to send back.[25]

James Bond has better luck with the pâté in the film of *Live and Let Die* (1973). It's one of the items in the hamper that he shares with treacherous CIA agent Rosie Carver in the hills of Jamaica. He declares this one to be "excellent."

Traditionally, many restaurants, bistros and charcuteries in France offer pâtés made to the establishments' own recipes. The pâtés vary in flavour and ingredients, but generally contain some combination of lean meats, such as chicken, veal or game, and fatty pieces, such as belly pork or bacon. Liver is usually included. Here's my recipe for a coarse pâté. I've used ingredients that were available to me at the time of cooking, but any of the meats specified can be substituted for others.

Makes several servings

4 oz./120 g. belly pork
4 oz./120 g. chicken breast (skin removed)
4 oz./100 g. veal liver
2 oz./50 g. cooked ham
2 tbps. white wine
1–2 cloves of garlic, peeled and finely chopped
Bacon rashers
Salt and black pepper

Heat the oven to 350°F (180°C; 160°C fan-assisted). Trim any excess fat from the belly pork. Cut the pork, chicken, liver and ham into pieces. Mince the meat in a food processor. Transfer the meat to a mixing bowl and add the wine, garlic and pinches of salt and pepper. Mix all the ingredients together. Put the mixture into a terrine or other oven dish, lay some bacon rashers over the top and cover the dish with foil or a lid. Place the dish in water-filled pan or bain-marie. The water should extend about halfway up the side of the dish. Put the pan into the oven and cook for 1¼–1½ hours. After cooking, remove the pan from the oven and let the dish cool. Refrigerate until required. Serve with a crusty baguette.

Peking Duck

Peking duck, a favourite of James Bond's, as mentioned in
the film of *You Only Live Twice* (1967). Photo: Author

When it comes to a choice between Russian caviar and Peking
duck, James Bond (Sean Connery) doesn't have a preference.
As he tells his companion, Ling (Tsai Chin), at the start of *You
Only Live Twice* (1967), he loves them both. One is not better
than the other, they just taste different. Like Chinese girls and all
other girls. Ling promises Bond the very best duck, which Bond
thinks would be lovely, at which moment he is unceremoniously
machine-gunned in his bed. A ruse, thankfully, but he never did
get that duck.

Ian Fleming was also fond of Peking duck. As recorded in
Thrilling Cities (1963), he sampled the dish at the Peking Restaurant during a visit to Hong Kong with Richard Hughes, the *Sunday
Times'* Far Eastern correspondent. The duck was accompanied by
shark's fin soup, shrimp balls, bamboo shoots with seaweed, and
chicken and walnuts, and Fleming thought the meal was "in every
respect delicious."[26]

My recipe includes two ingredients that give the dish a Bondian twist: vodka martini and one of Bond's breakfast items, heather honey. The martini is unusual, I'll admit, but, as explained below, it helps with the preparation of the duck before cooking. As for the honey, this is a typical ingredient in the dish, so why not use Bond's favourite type?

Serves 3–4

    1 duck
    1 vodka martini (3 measures vodka, ½ measure dry vermouth)
    3 tbsp. dark soy sauce
    3 tbsp. heather honey (preferably Norwegian)
    1 tsp. Chinese five spice powder
    ⅝ cup/150 ml. water
    A further 150ml water for cooking

When cooking Peking duck, the secret of a crispy skin is to dry the skin thoroughly before cooking. Traditionally, when making the dish in the home, the duck is suspended between two chairs and dried over several hours by means of electric fan, bicycle pumps, or a breeze coming through the window. I managed to achieve a dry skin, slightly leathery to the touch, by placing the duck uncovered on the worktop and, overnight, in the refrigerator, over a 24-hour period.

It's said that rubbing the skin with brandy, vodka or some similar spirit aids the drying process, and so naturally I brushed the skin at the beginning of the drying with a vodka martini, using the ratio specified in the novel of *Live and Let Die* (1954).

However you dry the skin of the duck, when it's ready for the oven, make a basting sauce by putting the soy sauce, honey, Chinese five spice powder, and water into a small saucepan, placing the pan over a high heat, and stirring until the ingredients are well combined. (There's no need to bring the mixture to the boil.)

Heat the oven to 475°F (240°C; 220°C fan-assisted). Put the duck on a wire rack, placing the rack in turn into a roasting pan. Pour ⅝ cup/150 ml. of water into the pan. Brush the basting sauce all over the skin of the duck and put the pan in the oven.

Cook for 15 minutes, then turn the oven temperature down to 350°F (180°C; 160°C fan-assisted). Take the duck out of the oven, baste it with the sauce, then put the duck back in the oven. Cook for a further 1¼ hours, basting every 20 minutes or so.

At the end of the cooking time, remove the duck from the oven, then let it rest for 10 minutes. Slice or shred the duck and serve it with pancakes, sliced cucumber and spring onions, and hoisin sauce.

Poularde à la Crème

James Bond is disappointed with his evening meal at an auberge on the south bank of the Loire, as revealed in the novel of *On Her Majesty's Secret Service* (1963). Noticing that the establishment is decorated with faux antiques, he decides that his poularde à la crème is the only genuine antique in the place.[27] A poularde is a fattened young hen. In France it is traditionally available at Christmas, and so to have it on the menu in September, when Bond's adventure begins, suggests that the bird is an old one, hence Bond's comment. Even now, one would be hard-pressed to find poulardes on the supermarket shelves, but this recipe works equally well with an ordinary chicken, in which case it becomes poulet à la crème.

Serves 3–4

1 poularde (or chicken)
1 onion, chopped
1 stick of celery, sliced
1 bay leaf
⅝ cup/150 ml. chicken stock

⅝ cup/150 ml. dry white wine (preferably from the Loire region)
Black pepper
1 tbsp. vegetable oil
For the sauce:
2 egg yolks
6 oz./170 ml. double cream
1 tsp. tarragon, finely chopped

Chop the poularde (or ordinary chicken) into eight pieces—two legs, two thighs and four breast pieces. Heat the oil in a deep frying pan or saucepan and fry the onion and celery until soft, then add the chicken pieces. Brown the pieces over a medium heat for about 5 minutes, turning once. Add the stock, wine, bay leaf and a pinch of pepper, cover the pan with a lid, turn the heat to low and cook the chicken for about 30 minutes. Check that the meat is cooked through (if not, continue cooking for another 5 minutes). Transfer the chicken pieces to a serving dish and keep warm.

Strain the liquid, then return it to the pan. Reduce the liquid approximately by half over a high heat. Meanwhile, whisk the egg yolks and cream together in a bowl, ensuring that they are well combined. Mix in 2 or 3 tablespoons of the pan liquid. Take the pan off the heat, and gradually stir in the egg and cream mixture. Place the pan over a very low heat and continue to stir the sauce until it has thickened (removing the pan off the heat if the sauce begins to boil). Return the chicken pieces to the pan and cover them with the sauce. Sprinkle the tarragon over the top and serve.

Rib of Beef with Red Wine Jus

It's lunchtime in Miami early on in the novel of *Goldfinger* (1959), and Bond has a few hours to spare before returning to investigate Goldfinger's rather unorthodox canasta play. The lunch is not insubstantial—a four-course meal beginning with a shrimp cocktail, followed by snapper with tartare sauce, prime rib of beef au jus, and, to finish, pineapple surprise.[28] After this feast, Bond crawls into his bed for a siesta, and who can blame him?

James Bond (Sean Connery) has the opportunity to have a similar meal onboard an ocean liner in the film of *Diamonds Are Forever* (1971), in which he is offered by Blofeld's hitmen Wint and Kidd (Bruce Glover and Putter Smith) a seafood course (Oysters Andaluz), prime ribs au jus, and (the pièce de résistance), la bombe surprise, made with real bomb.

Here's a recipe for the beef.

Serves 2–3

2 lb./1 kg. prime rib of beef
Cooking oil
Salt and pepper
For the jus:
Juices from the roasting tin
1 cup/250 ml. red wine
1 sprig rosemary
1 oz./20 g. butter
Black pepper

Heat the oven to 350°F (180°C; 160°C fan-assisted). Place a large frying pan or griddle pan on the heat, adding a tablespoon or two of oil. When the pan begins to smoke, lay the joint onto it and seal the surfaces and edges of the beef, cooking for 3 or 4 minutes overall. Transfer the meat to a roasting tin, season with a good pinch of salt and peppers and put it into the oven. For rare, cook for approximately 1 hour 20 minutes, and 1½ hours for medium rare. Remove from the oven and place the joint on a meat dish to rest for 15–20 minutes.

Use the meat juices that have collected in the roasting tin for the jus. As the meat rests, finely chop the rosemary, then place the roasting tin with the juices in over a high flame. (If preferred, transfer the juices to a saucepan.) As the juices start to bubble and smoke, pour in the wine to deglaze the pan. Stir the liquid, scraping the bits of meat off the bottom of the tin. Add the rosemary and season with pepper.

Let the sauce bubble furiously, continuing to stir. Add the butter and mix it into the sauce as it melts. Continue to cook until the sauce has reduced by half and has thickened a little.

Slice the meat as required, serve, and spoon the jus on and around the meat.

Roast Grouse

To celebrate his promotion in the novel of *You Only Live Twice* (1964) to the Diplomatic Section (and not getting the boot following his recent poor performance at work), James Bond decides to take his secretary Mary Goodnight out to dinner at Scott's restaurant in London for their first roast grouse of the season,[29] thus placing the start of Ian Fleming's eleventh James Bond adventure in August.

Scott's was, when the novel was written, located at Coventry Street in London, moving in 1967 to Mount Street. It remains there today. It was one of Ian Fleming's favourite haunts and he would often have lunch there. Though Scott's was known as a seafood restaurant, Fleming wasn't averse to ordering scrambled eggs, and clearly the restaurant had other items on the menu, including grouse.

When roasting grouse, it is best to use young grouse; older birds are usually braised, rather than roasted. Preparing the dish, the trimmings are perhaps more involved than the bird itself. Traditionally, roast grouse is served on a slice of fried bread and accompanied by watercress, bread sauce and toasted breadcrumbs. The instructions below draw on recipes first published before or around the time of Fleming's novel but include a twist or two.[30]

Per person

1 oven-ready grouse
3–4 rashers of streaky bacon
Generous knob of soft butter
Salt and pepper
1 tsp. flour
For the bread sauce (serves 2):
1¼ cups/300 ml. milk
2–3 baby onions (or 1 larger one), peeled and studded with cloves
2 oz./ 50 g. breadcrumbs (approx. 1½ slices bread)
1 oz./25 g. butter
Other ingredients (serves 2):
1½ oz./30 g. breadcrumbs (approx. 1 slice bread)
2 slices of brioche loaf
Salad leaves, including watercress

Heat the oven to 430°F (220°C/200°C fan-assisted). Season the soft butter and brush the butter generously over the breast and legs of the grouse and inside the cavity. Cut the rashers of bacon in half width-wise and lay the halves over the top of the bird, covering the breast and legs. Put the grouse in a roasting tin and cook in the oven for 40–45 minutes. After 30 minutes, take the bird out of the oven and remove the bacon and set it aside. Sprinkle the flour over the top of the grouse and put it back in the oven for the remaining cooking time. When the grouse is cooked (checking that the juices run clear), leave it to rest for five minutes or so while you finish preparing the trimmings. Don't switch off the oven quite yet.

Start preparing the bread sauce as soon as you've put the grouse in the oven. Pour the milk in a saucepan and drop in the onions. Over a medium flame, heat the milk, removing it from the heat as it begins to bubble up. Allow the milk and onions to stand for half an hour. During the last 5–10 minutes that the grouse is cooking, take the onions out of the milk and put the milk back on the heat. Add the 2 oz./50 g. of breadcrumbs and butter and stir until the sauce is bubbling away and becomes thick and smooth(ish).

While the bird is resting after cooking, butter the slices of brioche on both sides and place on a baking tray. Spread the remaining breadcrumbs on the tray at the same time. Place the tray in the oven and bake for about 5–8 minutes. (This method is a little healthier than frying but the result is just as good.)

To serve, place the baked brioche slice on a plate. Cut the grouse in half lengthwise, and lay the halves on the bread. Arrange the salad leaves and bacon around the grouse, and if desired, garnish the top of the bird with some of the leaves. Spoon the bread sauce and breadcrumbs into small individual-sized bowls or ramekins. If you want, you could dress the leaves with James Bond's dressing (see page 138).

The dish should also be served with "game chips", which are fried potatoes. I like to parboil potato "rounds", a quarter of an inch thick, for 5–7 minutes, then drain them, coat them in vegetable oil, salt and pepper, arrange them on a baking tray and roast them in the oven for 30 minutes. If cooking the potatoes in this way, start preparing them as soon as the grouse is in the oven.

Roast Partridge

In the novel of *On Her Majesty's Secret Service* (1963), James Bond enjoys half a roast partridge at Monsieur Bécaud's modest restaurant opposite the railway station at Étaples in northern France.[31] Appetites have grown since Bond had his partridge, so I suggest a whole bird per person instead of half. I wanted to incorporate something of the contemporary character and flavour of French cuisine into Bond's dish, and so I've taken my inspiration from a recipe published in 1966.[32]

Serves 2

   2 partridges
   2 rashers bacon

4 oz./100 g. seedless white grapes
1 tsp. thyme, finely chopped
Butter
Salt and black pepper

Heat the oven to 400°F (200°C/180°C fan-assisted). Rub the birds with the butter and salt and black pepper and lay a rasher of bacon along the breast of each.

After removing them from the stalks, wash the grapes, and mix them with salt and pepper and finely chopped thyme. Place the grapes into the cavities of the birds.

Place the birds in a roasting tin and cook in the oven for about 1 hour 20 minutes, or until the juices run clear. Rest the partridges for 5 minutes when cooked.

Shashlik

On board an ocean liner in *Diamonds Are Forever* (1971), Blofeld's killers, Mr. Wint (Bruce Glover) and Mr. Kidd (Putter Smith), enter the suite of James Bond and Tiffany Case (Sean Connery and Jill St. John) with a couple of trolleys laden with food and drink. It's a clumsy attempt to do away with Bond, but fortunately Bond smells a rat and turns the tables on his would-be assassins, who almost literally are given their just desserts.

One of the food items is shashlik, or shish kebab. At one point, Kidd arms himself with two flaming kebabs and approaches Bond. Bond throws the contents of a bottle of brandy over Kidd, who, having been set alight, hurls himself over the side of the ship. While the execution may not be well done, the lamb must certainly be. This is not the only time James Bond is served shashlik in the film series. In *Casino Royale* (2006), Vesper Lynd (Eva Green) asks James Bond (Daniel Craig) how his lamb was. "Skewered," he replies.

Makes 3–4 kebabs

1.3 lbs/600 g. diced lamb
1 large red pepper, deseeded and diced
1 onion, peeled and halved, then chopped into quarters
1 tsp. finely chopped marjoram
2 tbsp. white wine vinegar
2 tbsp. lemon juice
2 tbsp. olive oil
Generous pinch black pepper
Pinch salt

Place the lamb, red pepper, onion (separating each layer), marjoram, vinegar, lemon juice, oil, black pepper and salt in a mixing bowl. Mix the ingredients well. Cover the bowl or put the mixture into a large food bag and refrigerate for several hours, preferably overnight.

To make the kebabs, thread skewers alternately with lamb, red pepper and onion pieces. Place the kebabs under a hot grill or on a barbecue for approximately 15 minutes, turning occasionally.

Spaghetti Bolognese

Once, after a weekend visiting relatives who were vegetarians, I could think of nothing else but diving into the nearest fast-food restaurant for a burger, fries, onion rings, the lot. The food my relatives had served wasn't at all bad, but I began to crave meat and stronger flavours. That's probably the closest I've come to being James Bond. As described in the novel of *Thunderball* (1961), after two weeks at the Shrublands health clinic, fed an insipid diet of hot water and vegetable soup, James Bond fantasises about a large plate of spaghetti Bolognese to fill his empty stomach and revive his dormant sensations.[33]

Today, spaghetti Bolognese is a dependable mainstay of the domestic kitchen and student households the world over, its Italian roots long forgotten. In early 1960s Britain, however, the dish was exotic and suspiciously foreign. The first *Spaghetti House* restaurant opened in London in 1955,[34] just six years before *Thunderball* was published. It wasn't until after 1980 that spaghetti was included in the "basket of goods", the list of representative items and services bought by UK households that forms the basis of retail prices index and consumer price inflation index.[35] While a recipe for spaghetti Bolognese was included in Marguerite Patten's 1964 edition of *The Family Cookbook*, it instructed that the mere half to one clove of garlic listed "could be omitted."[36] For Bond, who longed for plenty of chopped garlic in his Bolognese sauce, the very idea would have been unthinkable. Tellingly, in the 2007 edition, the measure of garlic had increased to two cloves and its inclusion was not optional.[37] A sign of changing times and tastes indeed.

The film series has a minor connection with the dish. During the filming of *The Spy Who Loved Me* (1977), producer Cubby Broccoli set up the "Trattoria Broccoli" and served spaghetti to hungry crew members, while Roger Moore served the sauce.[38]

Serves 2–3

    2 tbsp. olive oil
    7 oz./200 g. beef mince
    2 rashers smoked bacon, chopped
    1 x 14 oz. (400 g.) can chopped tomatoes
    1 medium onion, peeled and chopped
    1 small or medium carrot, peeled and diced
    3 cloves garlic, peeled and chopped
    ⅝ cup/150 ml. red wine (preferably Italian)
    1 tbsp. tomato purée
    2 tbsp. fresh basil, coarsely chopped
    1 tsp. fresh oregano coarsely chopped
    Salt and black pepper
    5 oz./150 g. dried spaghetti

Heat the oil in a large saucepan over a medium heat and fry the onion and carrot until the onion begins to soften. Add the garlic and bacon and fry for a further minute or so, then the mince. Brown the meat, gently breaking it up with the spoon or spatula.

Mix the tomato purée, oregano and half the basil into the sauce. Add a pinch of salt and a generous pinch of pepper. Add the tomatoes and wine and stir the sauce well. Cover, bring the sauce to the boil, then reduce the heat and let the sauce simmer for at least 45 minutes and preferably an hour to an hour and a half, stirring occasionally.

Towards the end of the cooking time, bring a large pan of salted water to the boil and drop in the spaghetti. When the spaghetti has softened into the pan, cover the pan with a lid, bring the water to the boil, then switch off the heat and let the pasta cook in its own heat for about 10 minutes.

Drain the pasta, tip it into the sauce, add the remaining basil and toss. Spoon onto plates and serve with a salad.

Spaghetti with Caruso Sauce

What do American gangsters eat? Spaghetti, according to James Bond in the novel of *Diamonds Are Forever* (1956). Felix Leiter thinks so too; after he and Bond arrive at the Pavilion restaurant in Saratoga, he hopes they're not going to be put off their broiled Maine lobster with melted butter by the sight of the Spang boys tucking into spaghetti with Caruso sauce at the next table.[39] It is claimed that Caruso sauce was invented in the 1950s in Uruguay by chef Raymundo Monti.[40] Given that Fleming's novel was published in 1956, this origin story seems a little fanciful, and indeed the sauce is demonstrably earlier. For instance, spaghetti à la Caruso appears on a 1948 menu issued by Pomeroy's Restaurant in the United States,[41] and there may be earlier menus still. There are many variations of the sauce. Here is my version.

Serves 2

5 oz./150 g. dried spaghetti
2–3 shallots, peeled and finely chopped
4 oz./100 g. smoked ham
4 oz./100 g. mushrooms, sliced
1 tbsp. finely chopped walnuts
⅝ cup/150 ml. double cream
1¼ oz./35 g. grated Parmesan
1 tsp. finely chopped basil
Pinch of black pepper
1 tbsp. olive oil

Bring a large, lidded saucepan of salted water to the boil, add the spaghetti, cover the pan, return the water to the boil, then reduce the heat and let the water simmer for 10 minutes or so until the pasta is cooked. (I tend to switch off the heat after returning the water to the boil. The pasta cooks just as well and in the same amount of time.)

As the spaghetti is cooking, heat the olive oil in a deep frying pan or saucepan and fry the shallots over a medium heat until they have softened. Stir in the ham and mushrooms and continue frying, stirring frequently, for a couple of minutes or so. Stir in the walnuts, pepper and basil, then pour in the cream and throw in the cheese. Mix the ingredients until they're well combined and continue cooking until the cream is heated through, the cheese has melted and the sauce is starting to bubble. Take the pan off the heat, then drain the spaghetti and fold it into the sauce. Serve.

Steak and Kidney Pudding

Steak and kidney pudding, knowledge of which allowing the
brainwashed James Bond gain entry to Secret Service headquarters
in *The Man with the Golden Gun* (1965). Photo: Author

If it's Wednesday, then steak and kidney pudding is on the menu in
the Secret Service canteen. In the novel of *The Man with the Golden
Gun* (1965), this is the information that James Bond, brainwashed
by the KGB and bent on murder following the events of *You Only
Live Twice* (1964), offers Captain Walker of the Liaison Section to
convince him of his identity.[42] While we have no evidence that Bond
ever eats steak and kidney pudding, he would have been familiar
with the dish from childhood. This is a school-dinner classic and
was, certainly at the time Ian Fleming was writing, a fixture on the
menus of top London restaurants and gentlemen's clubs.

Serves 2–3

For the pastry:
6 oz./170 g. plain or self-raising flour (plus 2 level tsp. baking
powder if using plain)
3½ oz./85 g. shredded suet

Pinch of salt
Cold water (3–6 tbsp.)
For the filling:
14 oz./400 g. stewing beef, diced
4 oz./120 g. ox kidney, coarsely chopped
Plain flour
Salt and black pepper
You will also need:
Pudding basin
Butter for greasing
Greaseproof paper
String

To make the pastry, put the flour (ideally sieved), suet, salt and baking powder (if using) into a mixing bowl. Add the water, a tablespoon at a time, and mix the ingredients together to form a dough (you may not need all the water or you may need a little bit more). Place the dough onto a floured surface and knead it until it is smooth. Put the dough to one side.

In another bowl, combine the beef and kidney and a pinch each of salt and pepper. Add a tablespoon or two of flour and mix until the meat is thoroughly coated. Grease the inside surface of a pudding basin with butter (this recipe is ideal for a basin of 2–2½ pints or 1–1¼ litres).

Cut away about a third of the dough. This will be used to form the lid. On the floured surface, roll out the larger portion of pastry thinly and to a sufficient size to line the pudding basin. Line the basin with the pastry, allowing the pastry to overhang the top of the basin a little. Fill the basin with the steak and kidney. (A tablespoon of stock, water or red wine can be added, but I find that the meat provides sufficient liquid.) Roll out the remaining pastry to form a lid and cover the top of the basin. Press the edges of the pastry to seal and remove any excess.

Loosely cover the top of the basin with a generous piece of greaseproof paper. Fix the paper around the basin with string. Place the basin in a large saucepan. Fill the saucepan with boiling water so that the water reaches halfway up the basin. Cover the saucepan with a lid and place the saucepan on the hob. Bring the water to a gentle simmer and allow the pudding to steam for about 3 to 3½ hours. Top up the water if necessary. Traditionally, the pudding, once cooked, is served from the basin and not turned out.

Steak Tartare

How does one maintain one's stamina for making love? The answer, Kerim Bey reveals to James Bond over lunch in Istanbul's Spice Bazaar in the novel of *From Russia With Love* (1957), is steak tartare, which Kerim apparently eats every day.[43] While its supposed qualities can be disputed (readers may wish to test the veracity of Kerim's claim), steak tartare is delicious and simple to prepare. In Kerim's version of the dish, the usual gherkins and capers are replaced by peppers and chives. The raw egg yolk comes as standard.

The very eagle-eyed among you—or more realistically those of you with your fingers on the pause button—may have noticed that the dish makes a fleeting appearance in the film of *Thunderball* (1965): it's one of the items on the menu James Bond (Sean Connery) picks up at the Café Martinique in Nassau.

Serves 1

1 beef fillet steak
1 tsp. finely chopped red pepper
1 tsp. finely chopped chives
1 tsp. peeled and finely chopped shallot
1 egg yolk
Black pepper

Mince the steak by hand: first slice the steak thinly, then chop across the slices. Turn the steak and chop again. Fold the edges into the centre of the steak and chop. Continue to chop after turning and folding the steak until it is reduced to a pile of short strands or grains. Fold in a pinch of black pepper.

Put the shallot, peppers and chives onto a plate. Build a neat hamburger-like pile (use a chef's ring if available) of minced steak next to them. Make a small hollow in the top of the steak and carefully tip the egg yolk into it.

Traditionally, the ingredients are combined by the diner at the table. Break the yolk and fold it into the steak. Place the shallot, peppers and chives on top, then fold those in. Serve with bread or french fries and a salad.

Stuffed Sucking Pig

During his pursuit of Scaramanga in a Jamaican mangrove swamp in the novel of *The Man with the Golden Gun* (1965), a wounded, hungry and slightly feverish James Bond allows his mind to wander. As his thoughts turn to food, he imagines all the dishes that might have been served at a lunchtime buffet that Scaramanga had promised. Among the items are stuffed sucking-pig with rice and peas. Too hot for the time of day, Bond considers, but a feast nonetheless. At the end of *Live and Let Die* (1954), Quarrel prepares sucking-pig for James and Solitaire, but we don't know whether it's been stuffed or not.[44] My recipe for stuffed sucking (or suckling) pig is based on a Jamaican recipe dated to 1965 and is therefore contemporary with *The Man with the Golden Gun*.[45]

Given that sucking pig may not be readily available on the supermarket shelves, I have adapted the recipe for pork loin. When preparing the recipe, I happened to cook a 2.2kg piece of pork, which serves 6–8 and is every bit a feast as the sucking-pig itself.

Serves 6–8

Pork loin joint
Salt and pepper
String
For the stuffing:
4½ oz/130 g. chickpeas, cooked
3 oz./70 g. breadcrumbs (approx. 2 slices of bread)
1 clove garlic, chopped
2 tsp. capers
6–8 olives
1 tsp. thyme, chopped
½ tsp. allspice
Salt and pepper

Heat the oven to 350°F (180°C; 160°C fan-assisted). Tear the bread into pieces and put the pieces into a food processor. Add the chickpeas, garlic, capers, olives, thyme, allspice, some freshly cracked pepper and a pinch of salt. Process the ingredients until they form a paste. (If no food processor is available, use ready-made breadcrumbs, crush the chickpeas, chop the olives and capers, and mix all the ingredients thoroughly in a bowl.)

Place the pork skin-side down on the chopping board or work-surface. Cut the pork in half lengthwise, starting from the side of the loin. Stop cutting just before reaching the other side and open the loin out like a book. Spread the stuffing mixture over the surface of the lower half and flip the other side back over, effectively creating a stuffing sandwich. Bring the two sides of the pork together and tie string around the joint to secure the sides and form a roll. Place the pork in a roasting tin, skin-side up, and rub salt and pepper into the skin. Cook the pork in the oven for 2–2½ hours, depending on weight.

When it is cooked, remove the pork from the oven and rest it for about 20 minutes. Serve with rice and peas.

Sukiyaki

James Bond enjoys this "highly-spiced stew", as Ian Fleming puts it, during his Japanese adventure in *You Only Live Twice* (1964). Kissy, who helps Bond infiltrate Dr. Shatterhand's castle and becomes his lover, adds her own special spices: powder of dried lizard and sweat of toad procured from a Fukuoka sex-merchant.[46] Whether these aid Bond and Kissy's love-life is unclear, but we should probably dispense with them when preparing the dish ourselves.

The dish is popular and different versions of the recipe can be found in many Japanese cookbooks. The recipe given here is inspired on one published in 1964, the same year that Fleming's novel hit the bookshops.[47] Traditionally the meal is prepared over a portable burner at the dinner table, with diners eating the food as it becomes ready. As food is taken, more is added to the pan until the ingredients are used up. I've selected carrots and leeks here, but other items, such as mushrooms and tofu are also ideal.

Serves 2

For the stock:
2 tbsp. soy sauce
2 tbsp. mirin (sweet rice wine)
¾ cup/175 ml. water
½ tbsp. sugar
Black pepper
Other ingredients:
1 lb./500 g. beef steak
5 oz./150 g. shirataki noodles
1 carrot
1 leek

Thinly slice the beef, peel and cut the carrot into thin slices or matchsticks, and chop the leek into small chunks. Boil the noodles and cool under cold water. Cut the noodles into 2–3 inch/6–8 cm strips.

Put the ingredients for the stock in a saucepan. Bring the stock to the boil, then transfer to a chafing dish set up over a portable burner on the dining table (a fondue set can be used instead). As the stock bubbles away, drop in a few pieces of meat, noodles and vegetables, stirring them round with a chopstick and serving once cooked.

Toad-In-The-Hole

The classic British dish of toad-in-the-hole, as recalled by James Bond in the novel of *Live and Let Die* (1954). Photo: Author

Luxuriating in his room in the St. Regis Hotel in New York in the novel of *Live and Let Die* (1954), James Bond's thoughts turn to the scene back in London: bitter weather, a cold office, and a sign outside the local boozer advertising "giant toad and two veg".[48] Toad-in-the-hole is a classic British dish of sausages encased in a fluffy Yorkshire pudding-style batter. Though Bond had not been tempted into the pub by the sign, his thoughts indicate that he is familiar with the dish.

Serves 2–3

6 pork sausages
2 tbsp. vegetable oil
4 oz./115 g. self-raising flour
1 egg, beaten
1¼ cups/300 ml. milk
Pinch of finely chopped thyme,
Pinch of finely chopped sage
Pinch of finely chopped parsley
Salt
Black pepper

Heat the oven to 375°F (190°C; 170°C fan-assisted). Grease the sides and base of a deep oven dish with the oil. Lay the sausages in the dish and place the dish in the oven for about 20 minutes.

While the sausages are cooking, prepare the batter. Put the flour into a mixing bowl. Add the beaten egg, a pinch of salt and about a third of the milk. Thoroughly combine the ingredients together with a whisk or fork. Whisk half of the remaining milk into the mixture, then add the rest of the milk and whisk until the batter is smooth (though don't worry if the batter is a little lumpy). Stir in a pinch of pepper and the herbs. Refrigerate the batter until it is required.

Remove the dish from the oven and pour the batter over the sausages. Put the dish back in the oven, increasing the heat to 425°F (220°C; 200°C fan-assisted) and cook for 20–25 minutes or until the batter has risen and is golden-brown on top. Remove the dish from the oven and let it stand for a couple of minutes until the batter has slightly come away from the sides of the dish.

Tournedos with Sauce Béarnaise

Tournedos, eaten by James Bond in the novel of
Casino Royale (1953), prepared for cooking. Photo: Author

What is the first evening meal that Ian Fleming describes in the James Bond books? The answer is a very small tournedos with sauce Béarnaise, and a single artichoke heart, which James Bond consumes in the restaurant of the Hotel Splendide at Royale-les-Eaux in *Casino Royale* (1953).[49]

The method for preparing the tournedos is inspired by a recipe submitted for inclusion in *Les Plats Regionaux des Buffets Gastronomiques* (1951) by one Monsieur Bouveret, the concessionaire of the railway buffet at Rouen,[50] less than 100 kilometres from Royale-les-Eaux (assuming the model for the fictional seaside resort is Deauville) or 160 kilometres from the town if Le Touquet provided the model.[51]

Serves 2

> 2 fillet steaks (beef)
> 2 rashers streaky bacon
> Large knob of butter for frying
> 1 tbsp. Calvados (or brandy)

2 pieces string
For the sauce:
2 tbsp. white wine vinegar
½ tbsp. tarragon, plus ½ tsp. more
½ onion, chopped
1 tsp. peppercorns
½ tbsp. water
1½ oz./30 g. butter
2 egg yolks
½ tsp. parsley, chopped
To garnish:
2 slices of bread
Vegetable oil for frying

Prepare the sauce first. Put the vinegar, onion, peppercorns and half a tablespoon of tarragon in a small saucepan. Heat on the hob, reducing the liquid by half. Strain the flavoured liquid into a bowl or basin. Half-fill the saucepan with freshly boiled water and put the pan on a low heat, bringing the water to a very gentle, almost imperceptible, simmer—ideally more steam than simmer.

Add the cold water, a small knob of butter, and the egg yolks to the basin, place the basin on top of the saucepan, and start to whisk. Incorporate the remaining butter to the sauce a small portion at a time and continue to whisk for about 7 to 10 minutes until the sauce becomes smooth, thick and creamy. Add the parsley and the rest of the tarragon. Pour the sauce into a jug and set aside.

Using a pastry cutter or chef's ring (3 inch/7–8cm in diameter) as a guide, cut a circular piece from each steak. Wrap a rasher of bacon around the side of each piece, securing it with some string. Heat the butter in a frying pan over a high heat and fry the meat for 3–4 minutes on each side, occasionally turning the steaks onto their sides to cook the bacon. Towards the end of the cooking, pour in the Calvados and (taking care as you're doing this) set it alight.

Once the brandy has stopped flaming, remove the steaks to a warm plate and allow them to rest.

Cut two discs from the bread so that they're the same size as the tournedos and, in another frying pan, fry them in a little oil until both sides are golden.

To assemble the dish, place a piece of fried bread on each plate. Top this with a tournedos and spoon the sauce around it.

Veal Escalope in a Creamy Mushroom Sauce

James Bond enjoys a delicious veal escalope on the Venice-bound Orient Express with Russian spy Tatiana Romanova and the Spektor machine in the novel of *From Russia with Love* (1957).[52] We're not told how the escalope is prepared, but knowing Bond's penchant for rich sauces, I've decided to smother the veal with a creamy mushroom sauce.

Serves 2

2 veal escalopes
5 oz./150 g. button or chestnut mushrooms
⅝ cup/150 ml. double cream
2 tbsp. parsley
Salt and black pepper
Cooking oil

Place the veal in a food bag or under a tea towel and bash with a tenderiser or end of a rolling pin to thin the meat out. Heat a tablespoon of oil in a frying pan and fry the escalopes for about 3 minutes on each side. While the meat is cooking, wipe and slice the mushrooms and chop the parsley finely.

Once cooked, remove the veal from the pan and allow to rest. Put the mushrooms in the pan—adding a drop more oil if necessary—and stir-fry until the mushrooms are almost cooked. Take the pan off the heat, pour in the cream, drop in the parsley, and add a good pinch of pepper and salt. Heat the cream through on a low heat, stirring to combine well.

Remove the pan from the heat. Lay the escalopes on a couple of plates and spoon the sauce generously over them.

Venison with Smitane Sauce

From a hotel in Munich during the events of the novel of *On Her Majesty's Secret Service* (1963), Tracy di Vincenzo calls James Bond ahead of their nuptials and mentions her wonderful evening meal of crayfish tails in a cream and dill sauce, followed by saddle of roebuck with a smitane sauce (Rehrücken mit Sahne).[53] James Bond must have felt quite envious; he'd had to make do with some disappointing ham and mustard sandwiches.

For the recipe below, I've used frying steaks for convenience, but if you use saddle of venison (roebuck if you can get it), which requires roasting or braising, put a tablespoon or two of the juices from the roasting pan into the frying pan and fry the shallots in this. The recipe for the sauce is inspired by a classic Craig Claiborne recipe, originally published in 1966.[54]

Serves 2

5 oz./150 g. venison frying steak
1 tbsp. vegetable oil
For the sauce:
1–2 shallots, finely chopped
¼ cup/50 ml. dry white wine
⅜ cup/75 ml. soured cream
2 tbsp. double cream
1 tbsp) butter
1 tsp. lemon juice
Pinch of black pepper

Heat the oil in a frying pan. Place the steaks in the pan and, over a medium heat, fry the steaks for 4–6 minutes (or 6–8 minutes for well done), turning them over regularly. Keeping the pan on the heat, transfer the steaks to a plate and allow them to rest for 5 minutes.

As the steaks are resting, put the shallots in the frying pan. Fry them for about a minute, then pour in the wine and add the pepper. Allow the wine to bubble away until it has reduced by half, then stir in the soured cream and double cream. Add the butter and stir again. When the sauce starts to bubble, add the lemon juice, stir, and take the pan off the heat. Strain the sauce into a bowl.

Plate up the steaks, perhaps slicing them in half for presentation and pour the sauce over the pieces.

Virginia Ham with Red-Eye Gravy

Unlike James Bond, who pecks at his poached eggs and eventually pushes them away, Commander Pedersen of the Manta, a US Navy submarine brought in to help catch Largo and find the remaining atom bomb that threatens the world in the novel of *Thunderball* (1961), has a great appetite. On the eve of an epic underwater battle, Commander Pedersen cheerfully orders a hearty meal of Virginia ham with red-eye gravy, apple pie and ice-cream and iced coffee.[55]

On discovering that the essential ingredient of red-eye gravy is coffee, I wasn't surprised that James Bond opted for poached eggs. In his place, I think I would have gone for something that's tried and tested too. However, having prepared and consumed the dish myself now, I can confirm that, together, the ham and gravy is a taste sensation.

First, the ham. Traditionally, Virginia ham is meat taken from the hind leg of a wild pig, cured in salt and smoked with apple and hickory wood. The ham is hung in the smokehouse to age. If

Virginia ham is unavailable, a good-quality salt-cured and wood-smoked gammon makes a fine alternative.

Red-eye gravy is made from coffee, which is used to deglaze the pan used to fry slices of ham. The inclusion of coffee sounds most improbable, but in combination with the ham, the resulting gravy somehow works. For my first taste, I dipped a morsel of ham in a cup of gravy and with trepidation lifted it to my mouth. Before too long, I was pouring the gravy liberally over my slice. Have a go—I think you'll be very pleasantly surprised.

Incidentally, my gammon joint was ready to cook when I bought it. Other joints may need soaking before cooking.

Serves 2

2 slices, approx. ½ inch/15 mm. thick, from salt-cured and wood-smoked gammon joint (or two gammon steaks, if preferred)
½ cup/120 ml. freshly brewed coffee
Pinch black pepper

Place a deep frying pan on a high heat. When the pan begins to smoke, add the two gammon slices. Turn the heat down to medium and fry with slices without oil for 5 minutes on each side. Once cooked, transfer the ham to a serving plate.

Keep the pan on the medium heat. Pour the coffee in the pan and scrape the fat and bits of ham from the base of the pan as the coffee bubbles. Add the pepper and allow the gravy to bubble away for about minute until the liquid has reduced by half. Pour the gravy into a jug or other suitable vessel. Serve the ham slices and pour as little or as much of the gravy as you like over the top.

5. Beans, Legumes, and Vegetables

Artichoke Hearts

James Bond orders just a single artichoke heart in the novel of
Casino Royale (1953). Photo: Clare McIntyre

Bond's very small tournedos, described in *Casino Royale* (1953), is
accompanied by a single artichoke heart.[1] Appetites were smaller
in the Fifties. These days a few more, four or five per person, are
required to make a meal. I would not advocate preparing the arti-
chokes from scratch, but instead recommend using tinned or frozen hearts.

Serves 2

11 oz./300 g. artichoke hearts, tinned or thawed from frozen
1 tbsp. lemon juice
1 tbsp. thyme
2 tbsp. olive oil
Salt and black pepper

Heat the oven 400°F (200°C/180°C fan-assisted). Drain the artichoke hearts and place into an oven dish. Chop the thyme and add to the hearts along with the lemon juice, salt and pepper, and olive oil. Mix well, then put the dish into the oven and cook for about 20–30 minutes.

Asparagus

While in New York in late July on the trail of a diamond smuggling racket in *Diamonds Are Forever* (1956), James Bond enjoys the last of the asparagus, which is normally in season from March to July or August. Bond's something of an expert in the vegetable, ordering it at a May-time meal at M's club in *Moonraker* (1955), knowing that it's during that time that asparagus is at its best.[2] James Bond has his asparagus with either a mousseline or Béarnaise sauce, but the recipe below offers simple, fresh, flavours that makes asparagus a wonderful accompaniment to fish or chicken.

Serves 2

9 oz./250 g. bunch asparagus
1 tbsp. lemon juice
1 tbsp. parsley
Black pepper
Olive oil for frying

Chop the woody ends off the asparagus spears. Boil the asparagus for about 5 minutes, until the pieces are becoming tender but there's still a bit of bite. Drain the asparagus and cool under cold water.

Heat a generous drizzle of oil in a frying pan and add the asparagus. As the pieces cook (turn frequently) add the lemon juice and a few twists of freshly cracked pepper. Finely chop the parsley and add to the pan. Stir the ingredients round and continue cooking until the asparagus is fully tender, about another 4 minutes from the start of frying.

Avocado with French Dressing

The avocado is so familiar to us as a starter or breakfast item that the thought of consuming it at the end of the meal seems faintly nonsensical, but there is method to the madness. Traditionally, savoury morsels are served at the end of the meal—think of M's marrow bone in *Moonraker* or Bond's angels on horseback in *Dr. No*—and with this in mind, James Bond's avocado with French dressing in the novel of *Casino Royale* (1953) and *Diamonds Are Forever* (1956) doesn't seem quite so odd.[3]

Per person

> 1 avocado
> **For the dressing:**
> 3 tbsp. olive oil
> 1 tbsp. white wine vinegar
> A little Dijon mustard
> Pinch of salt and black pepper

Combine the ingredients for the dressing and mix or whisk thoroughly. Cut the avocado lengthwise, remove the stone, and slice the flesh into strips. Prise the slices away from the skin and arrange on plates. Drizzle the dressing over the fruit and serve.

Avocado Salad

How does James Bond maintain a balanced diet during his missions? Have Quarrel, a Cayman Islander and Bond's right-hand man in *Live and Let Die* (1954), cook the food. One of the dishes Quarrel prepares is an avocado salad.[4] My version has been adapted from a Caribbean recipe published in 1946 and has a suitably tropical dressing.[5]

Serves 2

1 avocado
1 carrot
1½ oz./40 g. spinach
1½ oz./40 g. watercress
2 oz./60 g. white cabbage (raw)
For the dressing:
1 tbsp. white wine vinegar
2 tbsp. vegetable oil
1 tbsp. pineapple juice
1 tsp. lime juice
1 tsp. mustard seed
1 tsp. fresh coriander
Salt and black pepper

Wash, pat dry and coarsely chop the spinach and watercress. Finely chop the cabbage, and peel and grate the carrot. Transfer to a salad bowl. Cut the avocado in half, remove the stone, then scoop out the flesh into the bowl.

Mix the vinegar, oil, and juice in a small bowl or cup. Crush the mustard seed and finely chop the coriander, adding both to the dressing. Season with a pinch of salt and pepper. Pour the dressing over the salad, toss, and serve.

Bean Curd and Rice

The novel of *You Only Live Twice* (1964) sees James Bond embedded in a Japanese fishing village as he prepares to infiltrate Blofeld's castle. Bond's food here is simple home-cooked fare, with bean curd (better known as tofu) and rice being the staple diet. The only embellishment is a beaten egg, added by Kissy Suzuki as a rare treat.[6]

My recipe adapts a near-contemporaneous dish, published in 1963.[7] Aji-no-moto or monosodium glutamate is obtainable from online retailers or Asian supermarkets. Tofu of the sort cooked here has something of the texture and appearance of scrambled eggs, which must have been reassuring to Bond.

Serves 2

For the rice:
7 oz./200 g. sushi rice
1¼ cups/300 ml. water
For the tofu:
11 oz./300 g. block of silken tofu
2–3 spring onions
1 small to medium carrot
1 tsp. finely chopped parsley, plus a little extra for a garnish
1 tbsp. soy sauce
1 tsp. sugar
A pinch of aji-no-moto
A pinch of black pepper
1 tbsp. vegetable oil for frying

Wash the rice thoroughly. Put the rice in a saucepan, pour in the water, cover the pan with a lid and place over a high heat. Bring the water to the boil, turn the heat to the lowest setting and simmer for 10 minutes or until all the water has been absorbed. Remove the pan from the heat and allow the rice to rest (keeping the lid on) for another 10 minutes.

While the rice is resting, trim and chop the spring onions, peel and finely slice the carrot and drain the tofu. Heat the oil in a frying pan. Put the onion and carrot in the pan and stir fry for 2 to 3 minutes over a high heat. Reduce the heat to medium and add the tofu. Stir to combine the tofu with the vegetables. Add the soy sauce, aji-no-moto, sugar, parsley and pepper. Continue stirring for another 2 to 3 minutes until the ingredients are well combined and heated through. (If desired, add a beaten egg after adding the tofu.)

To serve, spoon a portion of rice into a bowl and pile the tofu mixture on top. Sprinkle a little parsley to garnish.

Borscht

Borscht, the famous Eastern European beetroot-based soup, has the distinction of being mentioned in two James Bond films.

In *The Living Daylights* (1987), the colour of the dish is alluded to during the Trans-Siberian Pipeline scene, in which James Bond (Timothy Dalton) places the apparent defector Georgi Koskov (Jeroen Krabbé) into a specially designed pig or scouring plug to transport him into the West. Pipeline technician Rosika Miklos (Julie T. Wallace) warns James Bond not to "open the valve before 100, or he [Koskov] will be borsch."

In *GoldenEye* (1995), the dish becomes a term of insult, as computer programmer Boris Grishenko taunts his colleague about cracking his password: "I made it easy this time. Even you should be able to break it, borscht-for-brains."

While no one consumes the soup in the films (or the books, for that matter), borscht is well worth preparing, being easy to make and very tasty. As with all "peasant" dishes, there are countless variations, but the version below is reasonably typical.

Serves 4

1 lb./500 g. beetroot, peeled and diced
1 onion, peeled and chopped
1 medium carrot, peeled and chopped
½ stick celery, sliced
4 oz./100 g. leek, chopped
4 oz./100 g. turnip or swede, peeled and diced
1 medium potato, peeled and diced
1 bay leaf
2 tbsp. finely chopped parsley
1 tsp. finely chopped chives
Juice from half a lemon
3 pints/1½ litres stock
1 tbsp. tomato purée
1 tbsp. vegetable oil
1 knob butter
Salt and black pepper
1–2 tbsp. soured cream

Put the oil and butter in a large saucepan. Place the onion, beetroot, carrot, turnip, celery, leek and potato in the pan. Over a high heat, stir the vegetables until they are coated with the fat and the onion has begun to soften. Pour in the stock, and add the lemon juice, tomato purée, a generous pinch or two of salt and black pepper, the bay leaf and 1 tbsp. of the parsley. Stir to mix well. Cover the pan with a lid, bring the stock to the boil, remove the lid, then allow the soup to simmer gently for about 40 minutes to an hour.

At the end of the cooking time, whizz the soup in a blender or food processer, and pour into a serving bowl or individual soup bowls. Swirl the soured cream into the soup and sprinkle the remaining parsley and chives over the top.

Broccoli Polonaise

Broccoli Polonaise, possibly eaten by James Bond
in the novel of *Live and Let Die* (1954). Photo: Author

New York's St. Regis Hotel plays a small role in James Bond's adventures. Bond stays there during the events of *Live and Let Die* (1954) and, among other goings-on, is treated to American cooking at its best: soft-shell crabs, hamburgers, french fries, mixed salad, broccoli, and ice-cream with butterscotch sauce.[8]

Ian Fleming's choice of hotel for Bond may not have been entirely random. The hotel played its part in the British war effort, being the scene of crucial meetings over lunch and dinner between MI6 station head William Stephenson and key individuals in intelligence, military or government circles, including Ian Fleming, who regularly met Stephenson during his visits to New York in his capacity of assistant to the director of Naval Intelligence.[10]

What sort of food was on the menu? The New York Public Library is home to a vast collection of historical menus.[11] Trawling through the collection, I've found several menus that are broadly contemporary with Stephenson's time in New York. These naturally reveal some of the food being cooked up in the hotel's kitchens.

For example, attendees of a dinner to celebrate the centenary of the publishing house G. P. Putnum enjoyed oysters, Madrilene (a cold tomato soup) with dumplings, filet mignon, green beans in butter, potatoes Macaire (a kind of fishcake without the fish), salade Flamande (a vegetable-based salad) and ice-cream. Green beans with butter and potatoes Macaire were also served at the annual dinner of the University of Michigan Club of New York in 1949; the vegetables accompanied breast of capon Bercy on ham with mushrooms.

At a lunch in 1933, salade Flamande was served with a mixed grill à l'anglaise. The meal also included broccoli Polonaise—broccoli with a crispy breadcrumb topping. Broccoli Polonaise was again on the menu in 1937 during the annual luncheon of the National Association of Book Publishers, where it accompanied grilled chops and potatoes au gratin.

While these menus are by no means identical, there are common elements, with salade Flamande, broccoli Polonaise and green beans with butter being something of a kitchen standard. One wonders whether William Stephenson's meals included these items. More to the point, did James Bond's meal include them? Apart from the hamburger, crabs and ice-cream, we know that Bond has a mixed salad and broccoli. It's notable that in the historical menus, broccoli Polonaise is paired with grilled meat. As Bond's hamburger is from the charcoal grill, it's reasonable to assume that, if the meal is based on one Fleming ate, his broccoli is prepared in the same way.

American recipes dating to the 1950s and '60s describe the Polonaise element as a sauce, but in fact more closely resembles a stuffing mixture.

Serves 2

1 head of broccoli or approx. 9 oz./250g broccoli florets

1 egg

2 oz./40 g. butter

1 tbsp. lemon juice

1–2 shallots or a small onion, finely chopped
2 tbsp. breadcrumbs
1 tsp. finely chopped parsley
Pinch of salt and pepper

Remove the florets from the head of broccoli. Steam or boil the florets until they are just cooked and still have some bite. Drain the broccoli, return it to the saucepan and replace the lid to keep the broccoli warm.

While the broccoli is cooking, put the egg in a small saucepan and cover with water. Bring the water to the boil, then boil the egg for about 7 minutes. Cool the shell in cold water, then peel and grate the egg. Put the egg to one side.

When the broccoli is cooked, melt the butter in a small frying pan over a medium heat. When the butter begins to brown, add the lemon juice and onion. Fry the onion for about a minute. Stir in the breadcrumbs, parsley, salt and pepper. Mix in the grated egg and continue cooking for another minute or so.

Transfer the broccoli to a serving dish. Remove the frying pan from the heat and spoon the mixture over the top of the broccoli. Serve as Bond has it: with french fries and hamburgers.

Crème Vichyssoise

What does the detective Achille Aubergene (Jean Rougerie) eat in the Eiffel Tower's famous Jules Verne restaurant in *A View to a Kill* (1985)? We know it's soup of some kind, as Roger Moore's James Bond tells a waiter, after Aubergene's unfortunate demise, that there's a fly in it. Precisely what type of soup, though, it is difficult to say.

The obvious choice would be cream of aubergine soup, but I'm not so sure this is correct. Apart from the fact that the detective's name is not actually spelt "aubergine" (the spelling "Aubergene" is used in the script), the soup is best prepared by roasting the auber-gine (eggplant) first, and the result is a concoction with a pale brown or purplish hue and definitely not the soup in the restaurant, which is white.

There are any number of French soups that are creamy and white in appearance, among them soupe de poisson and potage de bonne femme among them, and according to menus, soups that have been served at the Eiffel Tower include cream of mushroom soup, cream of cauliflower soup, and the improbable-sounding cream of corn and popcorn soup. However, I'm going for Crème Vichyssoise, a cold cream of leek and potato soup which isn't technically a French soup at all, but one invented by French chef Louis Diat at the Ritz-Carlton in New York in 1917.[12] It has, though, become famous around the world and is served at top restaurants. And, well, Crème Vichyssoise just sounds more Bondian than soupe de choufleur.

If a cold soup doesn't appeal (it is delicious, though), the soup can be served warm, in which case it becomes potage parmentier.

Serves 4

11 oz./300 g. white part of leeks (2 or 3 leeks), sliced
11 oz./300 g. potatoes (2 or 3 medium-sized potatoes), peeled and diced
1 stick celery, sliced
1¼ oz./35 g. unsalted butter
3 cups/700 ml. chicken or vegetable stock
⅜ cup/100 ml. double cream
¼ cup/50 ml. milk
Generous pinch black pepper
Pinch salt
1 tbsp. finely chopped parsley or chives

In a large saucepan, melt the butter over a medium heat. When it has melted and begun to bubble, add the leeks, potatoes and celery.

Stir to coat the vegetables in the butter and cook them for about 5 minutes, stirring frequently, until the leeks have begun to soften. Pour in the stock, add the salt and pepper, bring to the boil, then cover the pan and reduce to a simmer. Cook for approximately 20 minutes, by which time the vegetables should be soft.

Remove the pan from the heat. Pour the soup into a blender and liquidise. Return the soup to the pan, check for seasoning (if necessary, adding a touch more salt) and allow it to cool. Stir in the cream and milk until they are well mixed, then refrigerate the soup for 2–3 hours. Before serving, sprinkle some parsley or chives over the top. If serving the soup warm, gently reheat the soup after adding the cream and milk.

Cucumber Sandwiches

In the film of *Moonraker* (1979), James Bond (Roger Moore) meets Hugo Drax (Michael Lonsdale) while afternoon tea is being served. Drax regards the ritual as England's one contribution to Western civilisation, and, as in the best houses and hotels, the tea is accompanied by cucumber sandwiches and what appear to be cakes or biscuits.

We can perhaps see in the appearance of afternoon tea (and indeed Drax's residence, a French chateau rebuilt in California) a trace of M's club, Blades, where Bond is introduced to Drax in the original novel. We're told that club members who stay overnight are brought morning tea and a copy of the *Times* (freshly ironed) by the club's valets.[13]

As for the cucumber sandwiches, James Bond declines those as well. His views on cucumber sandwiches are less well known, although in the novels he is by no means averse to a sandwich (usually ham). The sandwiches in *Moonraker* are arranged neatly on a dish and appear clearly enough on the screen to help us recreate them at home.

To make cucumber sandwiches, peel the cucumber, slice it thinly, sprinkle a little salt and pepper over the slices, butter slices of soft white bread, remove the crusts, lay the cucumber on the bread (the cucumber slices may overlap to reduce gaps, but not be stacked), close the sandwiches and cut them into triangles.

Fried Mushrooms

Scaramanga lives rather well in the film of *The Man with the Golden Gun* (1974), enjoying as he does an island hideaway, a private funhouse, an (almost) impeccable wine-cellar, and the services of a Cordon Bleu-trained chef, who is of course his faithful manservant, Nick Nack. Among Nick Nack's creations is fried mushrooms, which Mary Goodnight, making stilted small-talk during lunch with Scaramanga and James Bond, says look "terribly interesting."

How would a gourmet chef such as Nick Nack fry mushrooms? Possibly something like the recipe below, which adapts a 1961 recipe by the French gourmet chef, Louis Diat.[14]

Serves 2

10 oz./275 g. sliced mushrooms
Large knob of butter
1 tsp. truffle oil (optional)
1 tbsp. finely chopped shallots or onion
1 clove garlic, peeled and chopped
1 tsp. finely chopped herbs (e.g. parsley, tarragon or thyme)

Put the mushrooms—when cooking this recipe, I happened to have closed-cup, chestnut and baby button varieties—without fat in a large frying pan, and over a high heat stir-fry the mushrooms for 2–3 minutes until they're more or less cooked. Tip them into a bowl and allow them to stand.

Place the pan back on the heat and add the butter and oil. When the butter is sizzling, add the onion and garlic and fry for 1–2 minutes. Meanwhile, strain the mushrooms—the initial cooking will have released a fair amount of liquid—then, once the onion has softened, return the mushrooms to the pan and sauté them for another minute or so.

Take the pan off the heat, sprinkle the herbs over the mushrooms, and serve.

Porotos

While James Bond may not often have time to sit down to a meal in the film series, food does crop up with surprising frequency. Take *Quantum of Solace* (2008). Following his exposure of Quantum members during the performance of Tosca, James Bond (Daniel Craig) crashes through the opera house's busy kitchen, causing food to fly. Then, outside the Bolivian bar where Bond meets Felix Leiter (Jeffrey Wright), there's a list of items painted on the wall. Three are shown: arvejas (peas), porotos (cranberry or borlotti beans) and lentejas (lentils).

I've created a dish using one of the items, porotos. Assuming the painted list refers to food available in the bar, I've prepared a sort of tapas dish inspired by Bolivian recipes that would go well with some rice or crusty bread and a bottle of cold Cervecita-like beer.

Serves 2

1 tbsp. olive oil
1 medium red onion, peeled and chopped
1 tbsp. white wine vinegar
1 large tomato, deseeded and chopped
1 (14 oz./400 g.) tin borlotti beans (c. 8 oz./235 g. drained)
1 tbsp. finely chopped oregano (ideally fresh)
½ tsp. cayenne pepper (or to taste)
½ tsp. ground cumin

Pinch salt

⅜ cup/100 ml. water or vegetable stock

Parsley to garnish

In a saucepan, deep frying pan or flame-proof casserole, heat the oil, add the onion and vinegar, and cook the onion over a medium heat for approximately 5 minutes or until the onion has softened. Spoon the onion into a bowl, then add the tomato to the pan. Cook for about a minute, stirring frequently, then cover the pan and, over a low heat, allow the tomato to continue cooking for another 5 minutes, by which time the tomato should have reduced to a paste.

Return the onion to the pan and add the oregano, cayenne pepper, cumin and salt. Mix well, then add the beans and stir. Pour in the water or stock, stir again, then cover the pan. Allow the mixture to cook gently for about 10 minutes (if necessary, turning up the heat slightly to ensure that the mixture is bubbling). At the end of the cooking time, the liquid should have been absorbed and mixture have become thick and gooey.

Transfer the mixture to individual tapas-style dishes and sprinkle some finely chopped parsley over the top.

Potato Salad

James Bond appreciates home comforts, and what could be more comforting than a plate of potato salad, which, as revealed in the novel of *On Her Majesty's Secret Service* (1963), is one of the dishes he lives on when in England?[15] For the inspiration for my recipe, I have looked to the queen of home cooking in 1960s' Britain: Marguerite Patten.[16]

Serves 3–4

1 lb./450 g. potatoes, washed, peeled and diced

2 tbsp. mayonnaise

1 tbsp. double cream

1 tbsp. chives, finely chopped
1 tbsp. parsley, finely chopped
Salt and black pepper

Boil the potatoes until they're just cooked through. Drain, then mix in the mayonnaise, cream, herbs and a good pinch of salt and pepper. Leave to cool, then refrigerate until required.

Rice and Peas

Rice and peas accompany the stuffed sucking-pig that James Bond imagines is being served at a lunchtime buffet while he is hunting down Scaramanga in a mangrove swamp in the Jamaican-set *The Man with the Golden Gun* (1965).[17] The two dishes are as inseparable as roast beef and Yorkshire pudding and could be considered among the national dishes of the country. Indeed, in an article published in 1947, Ian Fleming included roast stuffed suckling pig with rice and peas in a list of dishes visitors to Jamaica were likely to encounter.[18] The recipe here, like that for the sucking-pig-inspired roast pork, adapts a Jamaican recipe published in 1965.[19]

Serves 2

4 oz./100 g. split peas
2 cups/500 ml. water
7 oz./200 g. long grain rice
1¾ cups/400 ml. water or stock
1 tomato, peeled, de-seeded and chopped
1 onion, peeled and chopped
1 clove garlic, chopped
1 tsp. parsley, chopped
1 tsp. chives, chopped
1 tsp. thyme, chopped

Salt and black pepper
1 tbsp. vegetable oil for frying

Rinse the split peas, put them in a saucepan and add the water. Bring the water to the boil, then reduce the heat and simmer for 35–40 minutes. Drain the peas and set aside.

Put the rice in a saucepan, add the water or stock, cover the pan and bring to a vigorous boil. Keeping the lid on, remove the pan from the heat and let the rice stand for 12–15 minutes.

Meanwhile, heat the oil in a deep frying pan or large saucepan. Add the onion and gently fry it over a medium heat until it softens and begins to brown. Add the garlic, tomato, , chives, thyme and parsley and continue to fry gently, stirring frequently. When the tomato has softened, add the split peas. Drain the rice if the water has not been fully absorbed. Tip the rice to the pan and fold into the mixture. Stir in a generous sprinkling of freshly-ground pepper and a pinch of salt. Continue cooking and stirring until the ingredients are well combined and heated through.

Salad Dressing, James Bond-Style

The essential ingredients for salad dressing concocted by James Bond in the novel of *Moonraker* (1955). Photo: Author

James Bond is very particular about his salad dressings. In the novel of *Moonraker* (1955), after a long briefing in M's office, he pops down to the near-deserted officers' canteen and mixes a dressing of his own concoction to go with the salad he's ordered, which accompanies a grilled sole. We are not given the full recipe, but it includes mustard.[20]

James Bond does much the same thing in John Gardner's *No Deals, Mr. Bond* (1987), though this time he's in the more luxurious surroundings of Blades, M's London club. Bond again orders a grilled sole and large salad and, true to form, obtains the ingredients to mix his own dressing. This time, we get the recipe, which is essentially a variation of the classic vinaigrette.[21]

Personally, I'd reduce the salt and pepper (perhaps to a generous pinch each), but the mustard powder, though it seems more than ample, is not overpowering once combined with all the ingredients. Quite what the staff of Blades thinks about Bond's fastidious behaviour is anyone's guess.

Serves 1–2

½ tsp. ground black pepper
½ tsp. salt
½ tsp. sugar
2½ tsp. powdered mustard
3 tbsp. olive oil
1 tbsp. white wine vinegar
1 tsp. water

Put the pepper, salt, sugar and mustard in a small bowl and mix together. Add the oil, vinegar and water and stir well until a smooth liquid is formed. Pour over your salad and toss.

Savara Salad

James Bond (Roger Moore) doesn't neglect his vegetables when he orders bourdeto when dining with Kristatos (Julian Glover) at the casino in Corfu in the film of *For Your Eyes Only* (1981). His choice of savara salad, which appears to include tomatoes, spring onion and possibly a red pepper, is the perfect accompaniment. Mix those ingredients with some bulgur wheat and you have savara firingi-yan—a salad of Kurdish origin and a substantial lunch or supper dish on its own.

Serves 2

4 oz./100 g. uncooked bulgur wheat
2 salad tomatoes, cut into eighths
½ red pepper, diced
1 tbsp. parsley, finely chopped
1 tsp. fresh mint, finely chopped
1 tsp. thyme
½–1 tsp. chilli pepper, finely chopped
Pinch each of salt and black pepper
1 tbsp. olive oil

Put the bulgur wheat into a bowl and pour enough freshly boiled water or vegetable stock to cover the grains by about 1 inch/2 or 3 centimetres. Cover the bowl and allow to stand for approximately 30 minutes. When cooked (the liquid should be absorbed, but drain the wheat if necessary), fluff up with grains with a fork. Once the wheat has cooled, add the remaining ingredients to the bowl and combine well, then serve.

Steamed Courgettes (Zucchini)

In *No Time to Die* (2021), Q appears to be
steaming sliced courgette (zucchini). Photo: Author

Poor Q. There he is, in *No Time to Die* (2021), preparing a romantic meal at his London home, his date about to arrive any moment, when James Bond (Daniel Craig) and Moneypenny (Naomi Harris) appear at the front door with a data-stick on which they want him to work his magic. For Q (Ben Whishaw), it seems to be a case of no time to cook.

What had Q been cooking before he was interrupted? We know what vegetable he's having: a courgette (zucchini), which he slices and cooks in a bamboo steamer. Given the steamer and the Japanese stylings of the film, it's plausible that Q gives the courgettes a Japanese flavour, possibly something like my sauce recipe below, which is inspired by one from a Japanese cookbook published in 1956, not so many years before the publication of Ian Fleming's *You Only Live Twice* (1964),[22] on which the writers of *No Time to Die* drew heavily. If you don't have a bamboo steamer, then you can improvise, as I did, by resting a sieve filled with courgettes over a saucepan of boiling water and covering the pan with a lid.

Serves 2

> 1 medium/large courgette (zucchini)
> 1 tsp. red miso paste
> 1 tsp. sugar
> 1 tsp. white wine vinegar
> 3–5 dashes fish sauce
> 1 tsp. mustard powder
> Pinch finely chopped parsley

Rinse the courgette, then chop it into slices 1 cm/¼ inch thick. Put the courgette in a steamer and steam-cook for 5 minutes. As the courgette is cooking, make the sauce by mixing together in a small bowl the miso paste, sugar, vinegar, fish sauce and mustard powder. Once cooked, tip the courgette slices into a bowl and mix in the sauce until the slices are well covered. Sprinkle the parsley over the top and serve.

Tagliatelle Verdi with Genoese Sauce

Dining with Kristatos in the short story "Risico" (1960), James Bond orders tagliatelle verdi with a Genoese sauce, which is described as improbably concocted from basil, garlic and fir cones.[23] The sauce is better known as pesto, which, though a common sight on supermarket shelves, is still best prepared fresh.

Serves 2

7 oz./200 g. tagliatelle verdi
For the sauce:
1 tbsp. pine kernels
1 large clove of garlic, finely chopped
1 oz./20 g. fresh basil, finely chopped
1 oz./20 g. Parmesan cheese, grated
¼ cup/60 ml. olive oil
Freshly-ground pepper

Bring a large saucepan of salted water to the boil. Meanwhile, crush the pine kernels in a mortar. Transfer the ground kernels to a bowl and mix in the garlic, basil, cheese and a pinch or two of pepper. Add the olive oil gradually and continue to blend. Alternatively, place uncrushed pine kernels and unchopped basil and garlic in a food processer along with the grated cheese and the pepper. As the ingredients combine, slowly pour in the olive oil. Set the sauce to one side.

Add the pasta to the boiling water and boil for 5–6 minutes until cooked. Drain the pasta and return it to the pan. Add the sauce and fold it into the pasta over a low heat for a minute or two until the pasta is thoroughly coated. Serve.

Vegetable Soup

James Bond's diet at Shrublands health farm, as described in the novel of *Thunderball* (1961), includes vegetable soup, which he takes every day at midday in a plastic mug.[24] The soup is something like the potassium broth that Bond learns about in *Nature Cure Explained* (1950) by Alan Moyle. The book, which seems to be the clinic's core text, is genuine and even has a recipe for the broth,[25] which I've adapted here. On Alan Moyle's instructions, I haven't included salt, and in fact the soup is tasty enough without it (despite its muddy green appearance), but you may prefer to add a bit of salt after cooking. By all means have some bread with the soup, but since Alan Moyle considers white bread to have little nutritional value, I suggest a few slices of rye or whole wheat bread.

Serves many

1 onion, peeled and chopped
3 medium carrots, peeled and diced
2 tomatoes, coarsely chopped
2 celery sticks, sliced
A handful (approx. 1 oz./20 g.) of watercress, coarsely chopped
A handful or two (approx. 3 oz./80 g.) of spinach, coarsely chopped
A bunch (approx. ½ oz./10–15 g.) of parsley, coarsely chopped
2½ pints/1¼ litres water

Put all the vegetables into a large saucepan. Fill the pan with the water, cover it with a lid and place it over a high heat. Bring the water to a boil. Remove the lid and allow the soup to simmer for 25–30 minutes. Pour the soup into a blender (in batches, if necessary) and blend until fairly smooth. Transfer the soup to a large bowl and ladle individual portions into mugs. Alan Moyle recommends that you do not gulp it down or take it too hot.

6. Fruit-Based Dishes and Desserts

Apple Pie

He may, in *Thunderball* (1961), be in a race against time to locate a stolen atom bomb, but the commander of the US submarine the Manta still has to eat. Preparing for an underwater battle with the forces of SPECTRE, Commander Pedersen tucks into a meal of Virginia ham, apple pie, ice-cream, and iced coffee, unlike James Bond, who's rather lost his appetite.[1]

In this recipe for apple pie, I've been inspired by a recipe for Vermont apple pie, published in 1957.[2] Apart from being more or less contemporary with the events of *Thunderball*, the recipe is an appropriate one for James Bond. Vermont is a state that Ian Fleming knew well. His friend, Ivar Bryce, whom he often visited, had a home there, and Fleming made Vermont the setting of the short story, "For Your Eyes Only" (1960). It's not improbable that Ian Fleming enjoyed a slice of apple pie while he was there.

The original recipe, said to be one of Vermont's oldest maple recipes, is unsweetened, since it is intended to be accompanied by maple sauce. Given that Pedersen has ice-cream with his pie, in my recipe, I combine the apples liberally with maple sugar, thus retaining the regional flavour.

Serves 4–6

For the pastry:
1 lb./450 g. plain flour
8 oz./225 g. butter

1 tsp. salt

4–5 tbsp. cold water

For the filling:

5–6 apples

3–4 tsp. maple sugar

In a mixing bowl, mix the flour and butter together with your fingers until the mixture resembles breadcrumbs. Add the salt, then sprinkle four tablespoons of water evenly over the mixture. Turn the mixture over with a tablespoon or knife, then bring it together with your hands to form a dough. If necessary, add a little more water. Knead the dough until it's smooth. Put the dough into a plastic food bag and refrigerate for about 15–20 minutes.

While the dough is refrigerating, heat the oven to 400°F (200°C; 180°C fan-assisted) and grease a pie dish or flan tin with butter. Peel and core the apples. (Place them in a bowl of water with some lemon juice to prevent the apples turning brown.)

Remove the pastry from the fridge. Cut off a third of it and put the smaller portion to one side. On a floured surface, roll out the larger portion so that the pastry is of sufficient size to cover the base and the sides of the pie dish, with a little overhanging. Roll the pastry around the rolling pin and lay the pastry over the dish. Prick the base a few times with the ends of a fork.

Dry and chop the apples into small chunks. Fill the pie dish with the apple and sprinkle the maple sugar over the apples.

Roll out the remaining portion of pastry. Lay the pastry over the top of the pie and crimp the edges of the pastry top and base together with a fork (or squeeze them together with your fingers). Remove excess pastry with a knife. Prick the pie lid with a fork and, if wished, brush the lid with some milk.

Place the pie in the oven for approximately 40 minutes. Once cooked, allow to cool for a little while before serving. Delicious hot or cold.

Green Figs and Yoghurt

Figs and yoghurt, James Bond's breakfast in both the book (1957)
and film (1963) of *From Russia with Love*. Photo: Clare McIntyre

Much to his surprise, James Bond rather enjoys this exotic breakfast of yoghurt and ready-peeled green figs, taken in an Istanbul
hotel in *From Russia with Love* (1957). He had feared that it would
turn into a fiasco.[3] As it happens, little could have gone wrong.
The yoghurt and the figs arrive in separate bowls and with nothing
added. We ought to follow this precisely, but why wait? The figs
deserve to be combined with generous dollops of yoghurt at the
earliest opportunity.

These days, figs can usually be eaten without peeling—just cut
away the woodier end if necessary. If the skin is a little tough, however, score the skin and place the figs in a bowl of freshly boiled
water and leave for a minute. Remove from the water and peel away
the skin.

Serves 2

4 fresh green figs
11 oz./300 g. Greek-style natural yoghurt

Honey (runny)
Pinch of cinnamon

Cut the fruit into quarters and arrange the figs in a bowl. Spoon large helpings of yoghurt into the centre. Drizzle the honey over the fruit and the yoghurt, and finish with a fine dusting of cinnamon.

Guavas and Coconut Sorbet

Guavas, a staple fruit of Jamaica, served with
coconut sorbet. Photo: Clare McIntyre

When James Bond eats guavas and coconut cream during his Jamaican adventure in *Live and Let Die* (1954),[4] the fruit is probably stewed, since this is how Ian Fleming usually ate it. Noël Coward recalls how, at Fleming's Jamaican retreat, Goldeneye, dinners inevitably concluded with stewed guavas and coconut cream, which, he claimed, tasted of armpits.[5] I don't think we need go to the trouble of stewing the fruit and risking the bodily aroma; ready-prepared tinned guavas will suffice. I'd also like to suggest another modification: creamy coconut sorbet.

Serves 2

14 oz./400 g. or 1 tin of ready-to-eat guavas
For the sorbet:
⅝ cup/150 ml. water
3 oz./80 g. caster sugar
¼ cup/60 ml. coconut cream
1 oz./20 g. desiccated coconut
1 tbsp. lemon juice
Garnish:
Sprinkling of desiccated coconut
Drizzle of coconut cream

Mix the sugar and the water in a saucepan and bring to the boil. Reduce the heat and simmer for 5 minutes.

Take the syrup off the heat and add the coconut cream, desiccated coconut and lemon juice. Combine the ingredients well, then pour into a container suitable for freezing. Allow the mixture to cool, then place the container in the freezer. Remove and break up the sorbet after about an hour and return to the freezer for at least another hour.

Drain the guavas. To serve, divide the fruit between two plates, placing the fruit on top of a swirl of coconut cream. Spoon the sorbet into a couple of ramekins and place them beside the guavas. Sprinkle the dried coconut across the plates.

Ice-cream and Butterscotch Sauce

James Bond's first meal after arriving in New York at the start of *Live and Let Die* (1954) is a feast of soft-shell crabs, hamburgers, french-fried potatoes, broccoli, a salad and, to finish, ice-cream. We aren't told the flavour of ice-cream—I like to think it's vanilla—but we know it's served with melted butterscotch.[6] We read that James Bond is happy with the menu, though is somewhat dubious about the butterscotch. A near-contemporaneous recipe for butterscotch sauce is included in *Harvest of American Cooking*, published in 1957,[7] and this has inspired the recipe below. While a thermometer is recommended when making sauces of this kind, my recipe, ideal for the agent in the field, doesn't require one.

Makes several servings

Ice-cream—flavour and amount to taste
For the sauce:
4½ oz./130 g. dark brown sugar
¼ cup/50 ml. water
⅜ cup/70 ml. Golden Syrup
¼ cup/50 ml. evaporated milk

Combine the sugar, water and syrup in a saucepan and place over a low heat. Stir continuously and gradually bring the mixture to the boil. Boil for about 8–10 minutes, by which time the mixture should have reached the "soft-ball stage" (a drop of the mixture should turn into a ball when dropped into cold water). Take the saucepan off the heat. When the mixture has cooled, add the milk to the sauce a small portion at a time and stir well until all the milk is used up and thoroughly combined. Drizzle the sauce over the ice-cream.

Key Lime Pie

Key lime pie, eaten by James Bond in John Gardner's
novelisation of *Licence to Kill* (1989). Photo: Author

In John Gardner's novelisation of *Licence to Kill* (1989), one gets
the sense that James Bond (Timothy Dalton) had been romanti-
cally involved with Felix Leiter's ill-fated bride, Della Churchill
(Priscilla Barnes). While on their way to the church, just before
drug lord Franz Sanchez almost spoils the party, James reminds
Felix (David Hedison) that he (Felix) is marrying an old friend
of his and that Della and James go back a long way. At the wedding reception, we learn something else about James: he is rather
partial to Key lime pie, regarding the dish as a wonderful palate
cleanser.[8]

As the name indicates, Key lime pie is traditionally made with
Key limes, fruit strongly associated with the Florida Keys, where
the opening sequence of *Licence to Kill* is set. As Key limes are not
commonly found on the supermarket shelves outside areas of cul-
tivation, ordinary limes can be used instead. For a twist on this old
favourite, the version below is more of a cheesecake in appearance
than a pie. The result, however, is just as delicious.

Serves 6

Juice and grated zest of 4 limes
9 oz./250 g. digestive biscuits
4 oz./125 g. butter
3 egg yolks
1 x 11 oz./397 g. can condensed milk
1¼ cups/300 ml. double cream
1 tbsp. icing sugar

Heat the oven to 320°F (160°C; 140°C fan-assisted). Grease the sides and base of a cake tin with some butter. Crush the biscuits in a food processor to create crumbs. Melt the butter in a saucepan over a medium heat. Stir the biscuit crumbs into the butter until they are thoroughly mixed. Spread the crumb mixture evenly onto the base of the cake tin and put the tin in the oven for 10 minutes. Remove and put to one side.

Whisk the egg yolks, ideally in the food processor, for about a minute (longer if by hand), then add the condensed milk and continue to whisk for another 3 minutes. Add the lime juice and zest (reserving a pinch) and whisk for another 3 minutes. Spoon the mixture into the biscuit base, gently spreading it to ensure an even layer, and return the tin to the oven for 15 minutes. Remove and allow the pie to cool (keeping it in the tin) for several hours and preferably overnight in the fridge.

Whisk the cream and icing sugar together until the cream is stiff. Spread the cream mixture evenly over the top of the pie. Carefully lift the base from the sides of the cake tin to remove the pie. The sides of the pie should be neat. Sprinkle a little of the reserved zest over the top.

Papaya and Other Fruit

Food is everywhere in the James Bond films, but you'd be forgiven for not always spotting it. Look closely whenever James

Bond walks into a hotel room, however, or sits down to breakfast, or the action moves to a kitchen, or a villain dines in opulent surroundings, and it's there: a bowl of fruit. Apples, bananas,
grapes, oranges, pineapples, peaches, plums—you name it, it's in
at least one film, adding colour and conveying a sense of luxury.
James Bond (Sean Connery) even eats a little of it, taking a grape
from a bowl of fruit in Shrublands health clinic in *Thunderball*
(1965).

Some fruits have a little more significance. Papaya or pawpaw
is a "Bondian" fruit in more ways than one. A papaya or pawpaw
forms part of James Bond's (Roger Moore) breakfast in the film of
Live and Let Die (1973). This is a nod to his breakfast in the original novel (1954), in which Bond eats a papaya with a slice of lime
for breakfast—along with a selection of other tropical fruit and the
inevitable scrambled eggs and bacon—during his first morning in
Jamaica.[9] In this, James Bond is following the tastes of his creator.
Papayas were a common sight on the breakfast table at Goldeneye,
Ian Fleming's winter retreat in Jamaica. During her visit to Goldeneye in 1948, Ann Fleming recorded how breakfast would typically
consist of pawpaw, Black Mountain coffee, scrambled eggs, and
bacon.[10]

Preparing the fruit is simple. When the fruit is suitably ripe (the
skin should retain an impression when gently squeezed), cut it in
half lengthwise, remove the seeds and any firmer flesh from the
centre, and then cut the fruit into convenient slices or scoop out the
flesh with a teaspoon. Large papayas serve two, the smaller ones are
good for one person.

Pineapple Slices

The humble slice of pineapple, full of enzymes that break down pro-
tein, is the perfect response to the richness of James Bond's main
course of lamb cutlets and asparagus with sauce Béarnaise at M's

club, Blades, in the novel of *Moonraker* (1955). Bond orders a slice of pineapple, but it arrives as thin slivers,[11] and that is how I have prepared it below. Not to be outdone by M's strawberries in kirsch, I've soaked the slivers in Armagnac. Any liqueur will do, but it's what I happened to have in my drinks' cabinet, and it's in keeping with the Cognac that Bond has after his meal.

Serves 2

   1 pineapple
   1 tsp. caster sugar
   2 tbsp. Armagnac (or similar)

To prepare the pineapple, cut off the top and bottom. Stand the body of the fruit upright, then slice the skin off thickly, so that the "eyes" as well as the skin are removed. Clear away the debris, then cut the pineapple in half lengthwise. Take one half and remove thin slices or slivers, slicing from top to bottom, working your way inwards until you reach the woody core. Put the slivers in a bowl, sprinkle the sugar over them and pour on the Armagnac. Coat the slivers well. Allow to stand for an hour or two. Repeat with the other half of the pineapple if catering for more than two people.

Plum Pudding

In the novel of *On Her Majesty's Secret Service* (1963), James Bond sits down to Christmas lunch at Quarterdeck, M's country home. The plum pudding duly arrives, flaming in the traditional manner. We aren't told whether he likes it, but he wistfully thinks of a ring for his betrothed, Tracy de Vincenzo, when M nearly breaks a tooth on a miniature silver horseshoe implanted in the pudding for good luck.[12]

Serves several

11 oz./300 g. dried fruit mix (raisins, currants)

2 oz./50 g. mixed peel, chopped

2 oz./50 g. glacé cherries, rinsed, chopped

1 apple, grated

1 carrot, grated

Juice and zest of a lemon

4 oz./120 g. plain flour

4 oz./120 g. suet

4 oz./120 g. dark brown sugar

3 oz./75 g. breadcrumbs

2 eggs

⅜ cup/100 ml. beer

¼ cup/50 ml. brandy

⅜ cup/70 ml. orange juice

½ tsp. ground cinnamon

1 tsp. salt

Combine the beer and brandy with the fruit and peel and soak at least overnight, but longer if possible, up to a week. Place the mixture in a large bowl with the other ingredients and stir until thoroughly mixed. Pour the mixture into a buttered pudding basin and cover with some baking parchment cut to size and then tin foil.

Place the basin in a saucepan and pour boiling water into the saucepan until the water level is halfway up the pan. Bring to the boil and simmer for 6 hours, topping up with water often, ensuring there is always sufficient water in the pan. Alternatively, place the pudding basin in a slow cooker, top up with boiling water, turn the cooker to high and cook for 8 hours.

Remove the basin from heat, replace the paper and foil with fresh sheets and store in a cool, dry place. When you wish to reheat the pudding, place the basin in a water-filled saucepan and simmer for about 2 hours. Once reheated, turn the pudding out and serve.

Salade Utopia

One of the more puzzling dishes offered to James Bond (Sean Connery) by Messrs Wint and Kidd (Bruce Glover and Putter Smith) on board the ocean liner at the end of *Diamonds Are Forever* (1971) is salade utopia. Your guess is as good as mine about what this dish comprises. It isn't something that graces the classic cookbooks, and my researches have drawn largely drawn a blank. It could of course be a dish in name only, a simple invention of the scriptwriters. One suggestion at least has been put forward, however. In his book *James Bond's Cuisine: Every Last Meal*, Matt Sherman describes salade utopia as a sweet dish of gelatine, pineapple and cheese.[13] Rather you than me, Matt. The thought of those ingredients together doesn't exactly set my taste buds racing.

That said, there is a tradition in French cuisine of gelatine-based salads; salade en gelée, for example, is a medley of cooked vegetables, such as carrot, green beans and celery, set in jelly.[14] Cheese and pineapple, too, are a classic pairing. Think of that archetypal hors-d'oeuvre of the 1960s' and 1970s' dinner party: cheddar cheese squares and pineapple chunks speared on cocktail sticks. Then there are those hallucinatory salads, also of the 1960s and '70s, consisting of cottage cheese, a variety of fruit, and a sprinkling of nuts, which were very much of their time.[15]

In that light, perhaps a pineapple-and-cheese-in-jelly salad doesn't seem so implausible, and it would be in keeping with the pink shirts, wide lapels, and kipper ties of *Diamonds Are Forever*.

Per person

    1 pineapple ring or 4–5 pineapple chunks
    2–3 tsps. cottage cheese
    1 tsp. chopped walnuts
    Unflavoured gelatine powder

Salad leaves or lettuce
Sprig of parsley

Prepare the gelatine as instructed on the packet. If using fresh pineapple, fry the ring or chunks for 2–3 minutes in a little butter and allow to cool.

Pour enough liquid gelatine into a ramekin, small dish or jelly mould to cover the base. Sprinkle the walnuts into the ramekin, dish or mould, then spoon the cheese on top, then gently place the pineapple on the cheese. If using a pineapple ring and the vessel isn't wide enough, cut the ring into quarters and arrange them over the cheese. Pour more gelatine into the vessel, filling it to the top and covering the pineapple. Place the vessel in the refrigerator and allow to set over several hours or overnight.

To serve, gently turn the salad out onto a bed of salad leaves or soft-leaf lettuce, and garnish with the parsley. Despite its dubious appearance, the salad is actually rather nice.

Strawberries and Cream

It's the end of the mission in *Casino Royale* (1953). James Bond has defeated Le Chiffre at baccarat, cleaning the SMERSH agent out. The game brings further rewards—the prospect of making love to Vesper Lynd and, as a prelude, strawberries and cream.[16]

I don't really need to explain how to serve strawberries and cream, but I thought I'd offer my version: crème fraiche with a vanilla twist.

Serves 2

14–16 strawberries, washed and trimmed
4 tbsp. crème fraiche
1 tsp. vanilla extract
Fresh mint leaves to garnish

Spoon the crème fraiche into a bowl, add the vanilla and beat until smooth. Divide the strawberries between two champagne goblets, top with the crème fraiche and add the mint.

Strawberries in Kirsch

While James Bond has some slivers of pineapple to finish his meal at Blades before pitting his wits against Sir Hugo Drax across the card table in *Moonraker* (1955), M opts for strawberries in kirsch (cherry brandy).[17] In the recipe below, I've included cream for extra indulgence.

Serves 2

> 14–16 strawberries, washed and trimmed
> 2 tbsp. kirsch
> 1 tsp. sugar
> Double cream
> Mint leaves

Put the fruit into a bowl. Add the kirsch and sugar and stir to coat the strawberries. Refrigerate the strawberries for about an hour.

Whisk the cream until it is stiff. Divide the strawberries between two plates or bowls, drizzling any remaining kirsch mixture over the fruit. Add a tablespoon of the whipped cream to each plate and garnish with the mint leaves. To complete the meal in true M fashion, follow the strawberries with a marrow bone.

7. Breads and Cakes

Café Complet

The site of the Hotel de la Gare, Orléans, where James Bond
stays in *Goldfinger* (1959). Photo: Author

Café complet is the classic French breakfast. It's simple, quick
and elegant, and has the distinction of being eaten both by the
literary and cinematic James Bond. In the novel of *Goldfinger*
(1959), having spent the night at the Hotel de la Gare in Orléans,
Bond begins his morning with a café complet at the railway station before continuing his pursuit of the eponymous villain.[1] In
the film of *On Her Majesty's Secret Service* (1969), James Bond
(George Lazenby) orders café complet for two at the Hotel Palácio
in Portugal.

The meal comprises a cup of coffee and a croissant, brioche roll
or large piece of a baguette, accompanied by butter and a selection
of preserves and honey. Fruit juice may also be served.

When travelling through France, I find that a croissant and chunky piece of baguette sustain me until the three-course "formule" at lunchtime. But this more leisurely petit dejeuner is perhaps not quite in the spirit of a café complet, which is a rapid affair for those on the go. Accordingly, James Bond's breakfast is likely to have been typical of a railway station bar—a croissant only, perhaps, to accompany his double ration of coffee.

Doughnuts

The James Bond novels don't just offer fine dining; some of the eating is very much "on the run". Let's take doughnuts as an example. In the novel of *Goldfinger* (1959), nurses distribute coffee and doughnuts to Goldfinger's associates ahead of their attempt to break into Fort Knox. In the novel of *The Spy Who Loved Me* (1962), a kindly police officer brings along coffee and a bag of doughnuts for Vivienne Michel after she escapes the clutches of villains Horror and Sluggsy at the Dreamy Pines Motor Court.[2] In both cases, the doughnuts are brought round in the morning. The implication is clear: for Ian Fleming, doughnuts are an informal breakfast item. Here's a recipe for ring doughnuts to have with your morning coffee.

Makes a good number of doughnuts

1 lb./500 g. strong white flour
¼ oz./7 g. dried yeast
1 tsp. salt
1¼ cups/300 ml. milk (warmed)
1 beaten egg
2 oz./50 g. butter (softened and cut into cubes)
1 oz./25 g. caster sugar (plus 4 oz./100 g. for dusting)
2 tbsp. cinnamon

Sieve the flour and place in a bowl with the dried yeast and salt. Make a well in the centre of the mixture. Add the egg, water and sugar and mix until a dough is formed. If required, add more flour. Add the butter gradually and mix until absorbed. Knead the dough on a floured surface until it is soft and smooth and not sticky. Place somewhere warm and prove until doubled in size.

Stretch out the dough, ½ inch (1 cm) thick, on a floured surface. Cut out circles using a doughnut cutter or alternatively use a 3-inch (8 cm) pastry cutter and remove the centre of each circle with a 1-inch (3 cm) pastry cutter. Remould the remaining dough and repeat the previous steps until all the dough is used.

Place the doughnuts onto a floured greased baking tray and prove until doubled in size. Remove them from the tray and, using a frying pan, fry in oil (¾ inch or 2 cm deep) heated to 350°F (180°C) for approximately two minutes each side or until each side is golden brown.

Remove from the pan and place on kitchen paper. Dust the doughnuts in sugar mixed with cinnamon and cool on a wire rack.

Garlic Bread

Ian Fleming was ahead of the curve when it came to food, anticipating culinary trends by describing, in his James Bond books, dishes and food items that had yet to be popularised. To a list that includes spaghetti Bolognese, curry and avocados, we can add garlic bread. Alas, there is no record of James Bond eating it, but in a December 1954 entry of his weekly "Atticus" column, published in the *Sunday Times*, Ian Fleming reproduced a recipe for garlic bread that he judged to be "sensational."[3]

Today a regular accompaniment to Italian food and many other dishes, garlic bread was, in the 1950s, a rare treat in the restaurant and almost unknown in the home (at least in Britain). Fleming's recipe, credited to Mary Crickmere, gave his readers the chance to prepare garlic bread for themselves and add a little sophistication to their evening meals.

The original recipe calls for what Fleming terms a "French roll" (obtainable, he says, from Lyons' Corner Houses). He may mean a baguette, but this in any case is what I suggest one uses.

Serves 2–3

    1 part-baked short baguette or baton
    2–3 fat cloves of garlic, sliced very thinly
    Softened butter

Heat the oven to 390°F (200°C; 180°C fan-assisted). Slice the baguette width-wise three quarters of the way through at intervals of about an inch (2½ cm). Butter the slices as best you can. You may have to push the butter in with the butter knife—don't worry if the top of the bread gets a little messy. Insert a slice or two of garlic into each slice. Put the bread on a baking tray and bake in the oven for 8–10 minutes. Remove the bread, cut the slices all the way through, remove the garlic and serve. Sensational!

Layer Cake

No, this isn't about the Daniel Craig caper that so impressed the producers of the James Bond films, but, rather, about the cake that's mentioned in "Quantum of Solace", one of the short stories in *For Your Eyes Only* (1960).

Not that we find out very much about the cake. Described as a "rich layer cake," it's served as the sweet on an Imperial Airways flight between Nairobi and London taken by Philip Masters, whose salutary tale the Governor of the Bahamas relates to James Bond.[4]

The orange cake described below might be the sort of thing that Philip Masters is served. In recognition of the Caribbean setting of the short story, the cake is inspired by a recipe published in 1962 in Jamaica's *Daily Gleaner*.[5]

Makes one layer

4 oz./115 g. butter
4 oz./115 g. caster sugar
8 oz./225 g. plain flour
1 level tsp. baking powder
3 eggs, beaten
Juice of 1 orange (reserving 1 tbsp)
1 tsp. orange zest
1½ oz./30 g. mixed peel
For the filling:
3½ oz./85 g. butter
6 oz./170 g. icing sugar, sieved
1 tbsp. orange juice
Zest of half an orange
¼ tsp. angostura bitters
For decoration:
Icing sugar
Dried orange slices

Heat the oven to 375°F (190°C; 170°C fan-assisted) and grease the cake tin. Cream the butter and caster sugar together in a mixing bowl. Add the baking powder to the flour and sieve the flour into the bowl. Stir in the eggs a little at a time, then add the zest, orange juice and mixed peel. Mix well, then scoop the mixture into the cake tin. Cook in the centre of the oven for 40 minutes. At the end of the cooking time, check that the cake is cooked and, if so, let the cake stand for about five minutes, then remove it from the tin and leave to cool on a wire rack. Repeat the steps to prepare a second or, if wished, third layer.

To make the filling, cream together the butter and icing sugar. Add the orange juice, the zest and bitters and mix well.

To assemble the cake, slice the top off the base cake, then spread the filling over the flat surface. Place the upper layer on top of the filling (or, if making a three-layer cake, spread another batch of filling mixture over the sliced top of the middle layer, then place the third cake on top of that). To decorate, put some icing sugar (about a tablespoon) into a sieve, then sprinkle the sugar over the top of the cake. Add the dried orange slices.

Pancakes

Pancakes, only the second dish that James Bond
cooks in the film series. Photo: Author

No Time to Die (2021) shows James Bond (Daniel Craig) doing something we haven't seen him do since 1985's *A View to a Kill*: cook some food, in this case French-style pancakes or crêpes. Well, we don't actually see Bond cook the pancakes, but from an open packet of butter on the breakfast table and a brief exchange about the food between him and Madeleine Swann's daughter, Mathilde (Lisa-Dorah Sonnet), at Swann's lakeside house in Norway ("pas mal" is Mathilde's verdict on the pancakes), the implication is clear. That's not the end of Bond culinary talents either: we also see him peel an apple.

Perhaps curiously, Bond cooks the pancakes for breakfast. While thick, American-style pancakes are a well-established breakfast food, wafer-thin, French-style crêpes are not. As the great French chef, Louis Diat, once wrote: "Breakfast is the only meal at which we French do not eat crêpes, even during Carnaval."[6] I also wonder whether the film's writers and director missed a trick here by not having Bond cook his signature dish in the novels, scrambled eggs.

To make crêpes yourself, try the basic batter recipe below, based on classic French recipes.

Serves 2

2 oz./60 g. plain flour
Pinch salt
1 egg
1 egg yolk
½ cup/140 ml. milk
1 tbsp melted butter
Butter for cooking
Lemon and icing sugar (optional)

Sieve the flour into a mixing bowl. Add the eggs and salt and mix until the ingredients are thoroughly combined. Pour in some of the milk and mix well. Add the melted butter and some more milk and continue to mix. Pour in the rest of the milk and whisk until you have a smooth batter. Allow the batter to rest for about two hours in the refrigerator.

To cook the pancakes, melt a tiny piece of butter in a small frying pan over a medium heat. Use a brush to coat the cooking surface with the butter. Ladle enough batter into the pan to cover the cooking surface very thinly, swirling the pan around to ensure an even spread. Allow the bottom of the pancake to cook for 30 seconds or so. When the top of the pancake looks dry and bubbles have started to form, flip the pancake over with a spatula or palette knife (or toss if you wish). Allow the other side to cook for another 20–30 seconds. If necessary, lift the edge of the pancake with a knife to check that the side is cooked. Slide the pancake onto a serving plate and cover with foil to keep it warm.

Repeat the process until all the batter has been used up. There should be enough batter for four or five pancakes, depending on the size of your frying pan. As the pan continues to heat up, the cooking time reduces; the last couple of pancakes will cook very rapidly.

Flavour the pancakes in any way you wish, but I like to go with the tried and tested, sprinkling the pancakes with lemon juice and icing sugar.

NOTES

Champagne, cards and chips: the essence of James Bond.
Photo: Clare McIntyre

How to Eat Like James Bond

1. Lyrics by Monty Norman
2. Fleming 1977b, 80 (Chapter 11); 1978a, 61 (Chapter 8)
3. Fleming 1978a, 60 (Chapter 8)
4. Moody 2013
5. Fleming 1978b, 9 (Chapter 1), 180 (Chapter 17)
6. Fleming 1978c, 20–1 (Chapter 2)
7. Fleming 2009, 408

8. Bryce 1984, 126; Fleming 1977d, 23 (Chapter 2)

9. Amory 1985, 64; Fleming 1978c, 20–1 (Chapter 2)

10. Fleming 1963, 66; 1978e, 188 (Chapter 22)

11. Fleming 1963, 101; 1977a, 118 (Chapter 16)

12. Fleming 1963, 119; 2008, 291

13. Amory 1985, 137

14. Fleming 1977a, 56 (Chapter 8); 1977b, 110 (Chapter 15); 1978e, 92–3 (Chapter 10)

15. Fleming 1977b, 45 (Chapter 6)

16. Fleming 1963, 101

Egg and Cheese Dishes

1. Fleming 1977b, 80–81 (Chapter 11)

2. Fleming 1978c, 111 (Chapter 11)

3. Fleming 1978a, 60 (Chapter 8); 1977a, 59 (Chapter 8); 1982, 42 (Chapter 5)

4. Brenner 1964

5. Fleming 1977d, 96, 114 (Chapters 10 and 12)

6. Fleming 1978b, 92 (Chapter 9)

7. Fleming 1977d, 23 (Chapter 2)

8. Fleming 1977b, 177 (Chapter 24)

9. Fleming 1962

10. Fleming 1978d, 212 (Chapter 22); 1978c, 136 (Chapter 14)

11. Fleming 1978d, 212–3 (Chapter 22)

12. Fleming 1978e, 98 (Chapter 11); 1978f, 82

13. Fleming 1978e, 89 (Chapter 9)

14. Fleming 1958

15. Fleming 1958

16. Chancellor 2005, 87

17. Amory 1985, 152

18. Fleming 2008, 291

19. Hellman 1961

20. Atticus 1955a, 2

21. Amory 1985, 137
22. Fleming 1980, 85 (Chapter 8); 1977d, 100 (Chapter 11)
23. Fleming 1977d, 142 (Chapter 15)
24. Fleming 1982, 124 (Chapter 17)
25. Lycett 1995, 195–6
26. Fleming 1978d, 181 (Chapter 18)
27. Fleming 1978b, 168 (Chapter 16)

Fish and Seafood

1. Fleming 1977c, 41 (Chapter 5)
2. *Jamaica Gleaner* 1979
3. Fleming 2008, 33, 53
4. Fleming 1977d, 203
5. *Michelin* 1958
6. Fleming 1953
7. Chamberlain 1960, 570; SNCF 1951, 95
8. Fleming 1978a, 60 (Chapter 8); 1982, 38 (Chapter 5)
9. Fleming 1978d, 113 (Chapter 11)
10. Gourmet Chef 1968
11. Fleming 1977a, 61 (Chapter 9)
12. NYPL, n.d.
13. Fleming 1978c, 121 (Chapter 14)
14. *Michelin* 1958
15. Fleming 2008, 269
16. Howe 1953
17. Fleming 1978b, 51 (Chapter 5)
18. Fleming 1978f, 159
19. *Jamaica Gleaner* 1964
20. Fleming 1977c, 35 (Chapter 4)
21. Don of Granada 1957
22. Fleming 2008, 222
23. Fleming 2008, 291
24. Fleming 1963, 119

25. Fleming 1977d, 24–25
26. *Michelin* 1958
27. Fleming 1977a, 65 (Chapter 9)
28. Chamberlain 1960, 187
29. *Michelin* 1958
30. Chamberlain 1960, xlii–xliii
31. Fleming 2008, 142–146
32. Fleming 1977b, 110 (Chapter 15)
33. Fleming 1978e, 133 (Chapter 14)
34. Fleming 1978f, 98
35. McBride 1957, 368
36. Fleming 1978c, 108 (Chapter 11)
37. Fleming 1982, 37, 39–40; Fleming 1977a, 59 (Chapter 8)
38. Atticus 1955b, 2
39. Amory 1985, 61
40. *Jamaica Gleaner* 1976, 26
41. Fleming 1978b, 9 (Chapter 1)
42. Fleming 1982, 124
43. Fleming 1977d, 23
44. Fleming 1978c, 120 (Chapter 14)
45. SNCF 1951
46. Fleming 1978, 21–2
47. Gardner 1995, 82

Meat and Poultry

1. Fleming 1977c, 123 (Chapter 14)
2. Fleming 1977a, 56 (Chapter 8)
3. Joy 1947, 10
4. Fleming 1978d, 123 (Chapter 12)
5. David 1970, 456; Reynolds 1966, 87
6. Wood 1977, 17
7. *Michelin* 1958
8. Fleming 1978c, 136 (Chapter 14)

9. Fleming 1977b, 113 (Chapter 15)
10. Fleming 1978b, 51 (Chapter 5)
11. Anon. 1901, 123
12. Field and Chowdhury 2015, 109
13. Wikipedia contributors 2021a
14. Fleming 1977c, 118 (Chapter 13)
15. Fleming 1978b, 9 (Chapter 1)
16. McBride 1957, 267
17. Fleming 1982, 37, 41 (Chapter 5); 1977c, 123 (Chapter 14)
18. Bond 1966, 35–6
19. Fleming 1978c, 125, 128 (Chapter 13)
20. Fleming 1982, 37–8, 42 (Chapter 5)
21. Fleming 2008, 108
22. Fleming 1977b, 127 (Chapter 17)
23. Orga 1958
24. Fleming 1978a, 45 (Chapter 6)
25. Fleming 1977d, 24 (Chapter 2)
26. Fleming 1963, 22
27. Fleming 1977d, 24 (Chapter 2)
28. Fleming 1978e, 32 (Chapter 3)
28. Fleming 1978c, 32 (Chapter 4)
29. Fleming 1978e, 32 (Chapter 3)
30. Anon. 1902, 91; Ceserani and Kinton 1990, 376
31. Fleming 1977d, 25 (Chapter 2)
32. Reynolds 1966, 94
33. Fleming 1978d, 37 (Chapter 4)
34. Spaghetti House, n.d.
35. National Archives, n.d.
36. Patten 1964, 12
37. Patten 2007, 128
38. Broccoli 1998
39. Fleming 1977a, 19, 102 (Chapters 3 and 14)
40. Wikipedia contributors 2021b

41. NYPL, n.d.
42. Fleming 1978f, 10 (Chapter 1)
43. Fleming 1977b, 113 (Chapter 15)
44. Fleming 1978f, 159 (Chapter 14); 1978b, 246 (Chapter 23)
45. Slater 1965
46. Fleming 1978e, 188 (Chapter 22)
47. Doi 1964
48. Fleming 1978b, 39 (Chapter 4)
49. Fleming 1978a, 60 (Chapter 8)
50. SNCF 1951
51. Biddulph 2015; 2020
52. Fleming 1977b, 184 (Chapter 25)
53. Fleming 1977d, 200 (Chapter 23)
54. Claiborne 1966
55. Fleming 1978d, 212 (Chapter 22)

Beans, Legumes, and Vegetables

1. Fleming 1978a, 60 (Chapter 8)
2. Fleming 1977a, 65 (Chapter 9); 1982, 37 (Chapter 5)
3. Fleming 1982, 42 (Chapter 5); 1977c, 123 (Chapter 14); 1978a, 60 (Chapter 8); 1977a, 59 (Chapter 8)
4. Fleming 1978b, 246 (Chapter 23)
5. De Brissiere 1946
6. Fleming 1978e, 135 (Chapter 15)
7. Froud 1963
8. Fleming 1978b, 9 (Chapter 1)
10. Hemming 2019
11. NYPL, n.d.
12. David 1970, 204
13. Fleming 1982, 25 (Chapter 3)
14. Diat 1961, 348
15. Fleming 1977d, 23 (Chapter 2)
16. Patten 1964, 54

17. Fleming 1978f, 159 (Chapter 14)
18. Fleming 1947
19. Slater 1965
20. Fleming 1982, 22 (Chapter 3)
21. Gardner 1987, 23–4
22. Manaolana 1956, 71
23. Fleming 2008, 108
24. Fleming 1978d, 27 (Chapter 3)
25. Moyle 1950, 82

Fruit-Based Dishes and Desserts

1. Fleming 1978d, 212 (Chapter 22)
2. Roberson and Roberson 1957, 210
3. Fleming 1977b, 99 (Chapter 14)
4. Fleming 1978d, 246 (Chapter 23)
5. Amory 1985, 55
6. Fleming 1978b, 9 (Chapter 1)
7. McBride 1957, 383
8. Gardner 1989, 10, 24
9. Fleming 1978b, 180 (Chapter 17)
10. Amory 1985, 60
11. Fleming 1982, 42 (Chapter 5)
12. Fleming 1977d, 183 (Chapter 20)
13. Sherman 2014, 80
14. Diat 1961, 400
15. Patten 1964, 53; Reader's Digest 1975, 108
16. Fleming 1978a, 60 (Chapter 8)
17. Fleming 1982, 37 (Chapter 5)

Breads and Cakes

1. Fleming 1978c, 120 (Chapter 12)
2. Fleming 1978c, 197 (Chapter 21); 1980, 163 (Chapter 15)
3. Atticus 1954, 3

4. Fleming 2008, 86
5. *Jamaica Gleaner* 1962, 16
6. Diat 1961, 426

APPENDIX: LIST OF JAMES BOND BOOKS AND FILMS

Recreating From Russia with Love: Turkish coffee, a Ronson cigarette lighter, and Eric Ambler's *The Mask of Dimitrios*. Photo: Clare Abbott

The James Bond Stories by Ian Fleming

Casino Royale (London: Jonathan Cape, 1953)
Live and Let Die (London: Jonathan Cape, 1954)
Moonraker (London: Jonathan Cape, 1955)
Diamonds Are Forever (London: Jonathan Cape, 1956)
From Russia with Love (London: Jonathan Cape, 1957)
Dr. No (London: Jonathan Cape, 1958)
Goldfinger (London: Jonathan Cape, 1959)
For Your Eyes Only (London: Jonathan Cape, 1960)
Thunderball (London: Jonathan Cape, 1961)
The Spy Who Loved Me (London: Jonathan Cape, 1962)
On Her Majesty's Secret Service (London: Jonathan Cape, 1963)
You Only Live Twice (London: Jonathan Cape, 1964)

The Man with the Golden Gun (London: Jonathan Cape, 1965)

Octopussy and The Living Daylights (London: Jonathan Cape, 1966)

The EON-produced James Bond films

Dr. No (directed by Terence Young, written by Richard Maibaum, Johanna Harwood and Berkely Mather, produced by Albert R. Broccoli and Harry Saltzman, 1962)

From Russia with Love (directed by Terence Young, written by Richard Maibaum and Johanna Harwood, produced by Albert R. Broccoli and Harry Saltzman, 1963)

Goldfinger (directed by Guy Hamilton, written by Richard Maibaum and Paul Dehn, produced by Albert R. Broccoli and Harry Saltzman, 1964)

Thunderball (directed by Terence Young, written by Richard Maibaum and John Hopkins, based on an original screen by Jack Whittingham and an original story by Jack Whittingham, Kevin McClory and Ian Fleming, produced by Kevin McClory, 1965)

You Only Live Twice (directed by Lewis Gilbert, written by Harold Jack Bloom and Roald Dahl, produced by Albert R. Broccoli and Harry Saltzman, 1967)

On Her Majesty's Secret Service (directed by Peter R. Hunt, written by Richard Maibaum, produced by Albert R. Broccoli and Harry Saltzman, 1969)

Diamonds Are Forever (directed by Guy Hamilton, written by Richard Maibaum and Tom Mankiewicz, produced by Albert R. Broccoli and Harry Saltzman, 1971)

Live and Let Die (directed by Guy Hamilton, written by Tom Mankiewicz, produced by Albert R. Broccoli and Harry Saltzman, 1973)

The Man with the Golden Gun (directed by Guy Hamilton, written by Richard Maibaum and Tom Mankiewicz, produced by Albert R. Broccoli and Harry Saltzman, 1974)

The Spy Who Loved Me (directed by Lewis Gilbert, written by Christopher Wood and Richard Maibaum, produced by produced by Albert R. Broccoli, 1977)

Moonraker (directed by Lewis Gilbert, written by Christopher Wood, produced by Albert R. Broccoli, 1979)

For Your Eyes Only (directed by John Glen, written by Richard Maibaum and Michael G. Wilson, produced by Albert R. Broccoli, 1981)

Octopussy (directed by John Glen, written by George MacDonald Fraser, Richard Maibaum and Michael G. Wilson, produced by Albert R. Broccoli, 1983)

A View to a Kill (directed by John Glen, written by Richard Maibaum and Michael G. Wilson, produced by Albert R. Broccoli, 1985)

The Living Daylights (directed by John Glen, written by Richard Maibaum and Michael G. Wilson, produced by Albert R. Broccoli, 1987)

Licence to Kill (directed by John Glen, written by Michael G. Wilson and Richard Maibaum, produced by Albert R. Broccoli, 1989)

GoldenEye (directed by Martin Campbell, written by Michael France, Jeffrey Caine and Bruce Feirstein, produced by Albert R. Broccoli, Barbara Broccoli and Michael G. Wilson, 1995)

Tomorrow Never Dies (directed by Roger Spottiswoode, written by Bruce Feirstein, produced by Barbara Broccoli and Michael G. Wilson, 1997)

The World Is Not Enough (directed by Michael Apted, written by Bruce Feirstein, Neal Purvis and Robert Wade, produced by Barbara Broccoli and Michael G. Wilson, 1999)

Die Another Day (directed by Lee Tamahori, written by Neal Purvis and Robert Wade, produced by Barbara Broccoli and Michael G. Wilson, 2002)

Casino Royale (directed by Martin Campbell, written by Neal Purvis, Robert Wade and Paul Haggis, produced by Barbara Broccoli and Michael G. Wilson, 2006)

Quantum of Solace (directed by Marc Forster, written by Paul Haggis, Neal Purvis and Robert Wade, produced by Barbara Broccoli and Michael G. Wilson, 2008)

Skyfall (directed by Sam Mendes, written by Neal Purvis, Robert Wade and John Logan, produced by Barbara Broccoli and Michael G. Wilson, 2012)

Spectre (directed by Sam Mendes, written by John Logan, Neal Purvis, Robert Wade and Jez Butterworth, produced Barbara Broccoli and Michael G. Wilson, 2015)

No Time to Die (directed by Cary Joji Fukunaga, written by Neal Purvis, Robert Wade, Cary Joji Fukunaga and Phoebe Waller-Bridge, produced by Barbara Broccoli and Michael G. Wilson, 2021)

BIBLIOGRAPHY

A tin of caviar, near-identical to the brand James Bond consumes in the pre-title sequence of *A View to a Kill* (1985). Photo: Author

Anon., 1901, *The American Cook Book: A Thousand Selected Recipes* (New York: W. R. Hearst)

Anon., 1902, *Mother's Cook Book: Recipes for Every Day in the Week* (Illinois: Homewood Pub. Co.)

Atticus, 1954, 'People & Things', *The Sunday Times*, December 19, 1954 (London)

Atticus, 1955a, 'People & Things', *The Sunday Times*, December 25, 1955 (London)

Atticus, 1955b, 'People & Things', *The Sunday Times*, July 31, 1955 (London)

Amory, Mark (ed.), 1985, *The Letters of Ann Fleming* (London: Collins Harvill)

Biddulph, Edward, 2015, 'Where is Royale-les-Eaux', *James Bond Memes: Exploring Bondian Ideas and Influences*, <http://jamesbondmemes.blogspot.com/2015/09/where-is-royale-les-eaux.html> [accessed August 14, 2021]

Biddulph, Edward, 2020, 'Le Touquet: The Final Model for Royale-les-Eaux', *James Bond Memes: Exploring Bondian Ideas and Influences*, <http://jamesbondmemes.blogspot.com/2020/03/le-touquet-final-model-for-royale-les.html> [accessed August 14, 2021]

De Brissiere, P., 1946, *Caribbean Cooking: A Selection of West Indian Recipes* (London: The New Europe Publishing Company)

Bond, Mary Wickham, 1966, *How 007 Got His Name* (London: Collins)

Brenner Felix, 1964, *500 Recipes for Cocktails and Mixed Drinks* (London: Hamlyn)

Broccoli, Cubby, with Zec, Donald, 1998, *When the Snow Melts: The Autobiography of Cubby Broccoli* (London: Boxtree)

Bryce, Ivar, 1984, *You Only Live Once: Memories of Ian Fleming* (London: Weidenfeld & Nicolson)

Ceserani, Victor, and Kinton, Ronald, 1990, *Practical Cookery*, 7 edn (London: Hodder & Stoughton)

Chamberlain, Samuel, 1960, *Bouquet de France: An Epicurean Tour of the French Provinces*, 6th Printing (New York: Gourmet)

Chancellor, Henry, 2005, *James Bond: The Man and his World* (London: John Murray)

Claiborne, Craig, 1966, *The New York Times Menu Cookbook* (New York: Harper & Row)

David, Elizabeth, 1970, *French Provincial Cooking* (Harmondsworth: Penguin)

Diat, Louis, 1961, *Gourmet's Basic French Cookbook: Techniques of French Cuisine* (New York: Gourmet Books)

Doi, Masaru, 1964 *Cook Japanese* (Tokyo: Kodansha International Ltd)

Don of Granada, 1957, 'Adventure in Foods', *The Sunday Gleaner*, March 17, 1957 (Kingston)

Field, Matthew, and Chowdhury, Ajay, 2015, *Some Kind of Hero: The Remarkable Story of the James Bond Films* (Stroud: The History Press)

Fleming, Ian, 1947, 'Where Shall John Go? XIII – Jamaica', *Horizon*, Volume 16, no. 96, December 1947, 350–59

Fleming, Ian, 1953, 'Diving Through Twenty-two Centuries: An Under-Water Report on Mediterranean Treasure', *The Sunday Times*, April 19, 1953 (London)

Fleming, Ian, 1958, '"The Exclusive Bond": Mr. Fleming on his Hero', *The Manchester Guardian*, April 5, 1958 (Manchester)

Fleming, Ian, 1962, 'How to Write a Thriller', *Show Magazine*, August 1962, 58–62

Fleming, Ian, 1963, *Thrilling Cities* (London: Jonathan Cape)

Fleming, Ian, 1977a, *Diamonds Are Forever* (London: Triad Granada)

Fleming, Ian, 1977b, *From Russia with Love* (London: Triad Granada)

Fleming, Ian, 1977c, *Dr. No* (London: Triad Granada)

Fleming, Ian, 1977d, *On Her Majesty's Secret Service* (London: Triad Grafton)

Fleming, Ian, 1978a, *Casino Royale* (London: Triad Granada)

Fleming, Ian, 1978b, *Live and Let Die* (London: Triad Granada)

Fleming, Ian, 1978c, *Goldfinger* (London: Triad Granada)

Fleming, Ian, 1978d, *Thunderball* (London: Triad Grafton)

Fleming, Ian, 1978e, *You Only Live Twice* (London: Triad Granada)

Fleming, Ian, 1978f, *The Man with the Golden Gun* (London: Triad Granada)

Fleming, Ian, 1980, *The Spy Who Loved Me* (London: Triad Grafton)

Fleming, Ian, 1982, *Moonraker* (London: Triad Grafton)

Fleming, Ian, 2008, *Quantum of Solace: The Complete James Bond Short Stories* (London: Penguin Books)

Fleming, Ian, 2009, 'Ian Fleming on Writing Thrillers', in Sebastian Faulks, *Devil May Care* (London: Penguin Books), 405–12

Froud, Nina, 1963, *Cooking the Japanese Way* (London: Spring Books)

Gardner, John, 1987, *No Deals, Mr. Bond* (London: Jonathan Cape)

Gardner, John, 1989, *Licence to Kill. From the Motion Picture of Licence to Kill Written by Michael G. Wilson and Richard Maibaum* (London: Coronet)

Gardner, John, 1995, *GoldenEye, Based on the Screenplay by Michael France and Jeffrey Caine* (London: Coronet)

Gourmet Chef, 1968, 'Split Pea Soup: Just Right for a Rainy Evening', *The Sunday Gleaner Magazine*, November 10, 1968 (Kingston)

Hellman, Renée, 1961, *Celebrity Cooking for You: Dishes Chosen by the Famous* (London: Deutsch)

Hemming, Henry, 2019, *Our Man in New York: The British Plot to Bring America into the Second World War* (London: Quercus)

Howe, Robin, 1953, *German Cooking* (London: Deutsch)

Jamaica Gleaner, 1962, 'Prize-winning Orange Desserts', *The Daily Gleaner*, April 26 (Kingston)

Jamaica Gleaner, 1964, 'Lobster Salad', *The Daily Gleaner*, May 19, 1964 (Kingston)

Jamaica Gleaner, 1976, 'Fat Fish: Good for Your Health', *The Daily Gleaner*, August 5, 1976 (Kingston)

Jamaica Gleaner, 1979, 'Ackee and Saltfish Duncan Special', *The Daily Gleaner Food Supplement*, September 27, 1979 (Kingston)

Joy, William, 1947, 'Brizzola', *Grosse Pointe News*, October 23, 1947 (Grosse Pointe)

Lycett, Andrew, 1995, *Ian Fleming: The Man Behind James Bond* (Atlanta: Turner)

Manaolana, Hui, 1956, *Japanese Foods: Tested Recipes* (Hawaii: Hui Manaolana)

McBride, Mary, 1957, *Harvest of American Cooking, with recipes for 1000 of America's favorite dishes* (New York: Putnam)

Michelin, 1958, *Michelin France* (Paris: Pneu Michelin)

Moody, Oliver, 2013, 'Marks & Spencer Serves Up an Exotic Dip into History of Taste', *The Times*, April 20 (London)

Moyle, Alan, 1950, *Nature Cure Explained* (London: Health for All Publishing)

National Archives, n.d. 'Consumer Prices Index (CPI) and Retail Prices Index (RPI) Basket of Goods and Services', *The National Archives*, <http://webarchive.nationalarchives. gov.uk/20160108054353/http://www.ons.gov.uk/ons/guide-method/user-guidance/prices/cpi-and-rpi/cpi-and-rpi-basket-of-goods-and-services/index.html> [accessed August 14, 2021]

NYPL, n.d., 'What's on the Menu', *New York Public Library*, <http://menus.nypl.org/> [accessed August 8, 2021]

Orga, Irfan, 1958, *Turkish Cooking* (London: Deutsch)

Patten, Marguerite, 1964, *The Family Cookbook in Colour* (London: Paul Hamlyn)

Patten, Marguerite, 2007, *Marguerite Patten's Family Cookbook* (London: Bounty Books)

Reader's Digest, 1974, *The Cookery Year*, 2 edn (London: The Reader's Digest Association)

Reynolds, Mary, 1966, *French Cooking for Pleasure* (London: Paul Hamlyn)

Roberson, John, and Roberson, Marie, 1957, *The Famous American Recipes Cookbook* (Englewood Cliffs: Pentice-Hall Inc.)

Sherman, Matt, 2014. *James Bond's Cuisine: 007's Every Last Meal* (Create Space Independent Publishing Platform)

Slater, Mary, 1965, *Cooking the Caribbean Way* (London: Spring Books)

SNCF, 1951, *Les Plats Régionaux des Buffets Gastronomiques* (Paris: SNCF)

Spaghetti House, n.d., "Our Story", *Spaghetti House*, https://www.spaghettihouse.co.uk/our-story [accessed August 14, 2021]

Wikipedia contributors, 2021a, 'Operations of KFC', *Wikipedia, The Free Encyclopedia*, <https://en.wikipedia.org/w/index.php?title=Operations_of_KFC&oldid=1035655683> [accessed August 13, 2021]

Wikipedia contributors, 2021b, 'Caruso sauce', *Wikipedia, The Free Encyclopedia*, <https://en.wikipedia.org/w/index.php?title=Caruso_sauce&oldid=1023969575> [accessed August 14, 2021]

Wood, Christopher, 1977, *The Spy Who Loved Me. A Novel by Christopher Wood Based on the Screenplay by Christopher Wood and Richard Maibaum* (New York: Warner)

INDEX

ABOUT THE AUTHOR

Edward Biddulph. Photo: Clare Abbott

Edward Biddulph has been a James Bond fan for decades. His earliest memory of James Bond is watching *Goldfinger* on the television aged 6 or 7. He graduated to the books aged about 11 or 12 and has been a devoted fan ever since. Edward has also been cooking from a young age. As a child, he'd often be in the kitchen, helping his mother with the cooking. Regular family holidays to France were culinary adventures, and over time Edward developed a deep knowledge of food and its preparation.

Away from James Bond, Edward is an archaeologist, a Fellow of the Society of Antiquaries of London, and the author of many archaeological monographs, papers, and reports. This academic side of his life, coupled with his interest in food and love of Bond, inspired him to research the food of James Bond and publish his first James Bond cookbook, *Licence to Cook*, in 2010.

Edward has written many pieces about various aspects of James Bond since then, contributing chapters to the volumes *James Bond and Popular Culture: Essays on the Influence of the Fictional Superspy* (ed. M Brittany; McFarland & Co.), and *The Many Facets of Diamonds Are Forever: James Bond on Page and Screen* (ed. O Buckton; Lexington Books), and articles for the *International Journal of James Bond Studies*, *MI6 Confidential* magazine and the websites *The James Bond Dossier* and *Artistic Licence Renewed*. Edward also maintains two blogs: *James Bond Memes* and *James Bond Food*.

CPSIA information can be obtained
at www.ICGtesting.com
Printed in the USA
BVHW031801160622
639860BV00001B/113

9 781629 339290